HOW TO GET RICH
BUYING BANKRUPT
COMPANIES

HOW TO GET RICH BUYING BANKRUPT COMPANIES

by Laurence H. Kallen

A Lyle Stuart Book
Published by Carol Communications

Library of Congress Cataloging-in-Publication Data

Kallen, Laurence H.
    How to get rich buying bankrupt companies / by Laurence H.
    Kallen.
        p.   cm.
    Includes index.
    ISBN 0-8184-0493-0 : $19.95
    1. Bankruptcy--United States. 2. Business enterprises--United
States--Purchasing. I. Title.
HG3766.K35   1989
658.1'6--dc20   89-32249
                                                                   CIP

A Lyle Stuart Book
Published by Carol Communications

Editorial Offices
600 Madison Avenue
New York, NY 10022

Sales & Distribution Offices
120 Enterprise Avenue
Secaucus, NJ 07094

In Canada: Musson Book Company
A division of General Publishing Co. Limited
Don Mills, Ontario

Queries regarding rights and permissions
should be addressed to: Carol Communications,
600 Madison Avenue, New York, NY 10022

Manufactured in the United States of America

Contents

III
BUYING OUT OF CHAPTER 7

IV
CONCLUSION

PART I

INTRODUCTION

Chapter 1

The Overview and You

Do you want to make money?

Money to give you options? Money to give you authority? Money to give you freedom?

Forget about becoming a rock star, stepping into Andy Warhol's shoes, or writing a best-selling novel. Do not bother staying up night devising a better mousetrap or finding the cure to the common cold. And, above all, stay away from Atlantic City.

The fast track to riches today is through acquiring businesses. The American economy has bounced back from its malaise of the 1970s with a vengeance. This has led to more opportunities for financial growth and diversification in the private sector. While the heavy hand of Big Business is, admittedly, still everywhere, the dynamic nature of technology and our economy makes it possible for small and mid-sized businesses to prosper. As a result, controlling an operating entity—a business—offers many opportunities to leverage capital through bank loans, earn a substantial income, and become well positioned to take advantage of other opportunities that come along.

Privately held businesses are very attractive prospects. While they may not generate the megabucks of the multinational megacorporations, it also takes fewer dollars on the bottom line to make their owners very well off. With proper management and capitalization, modest-sized companies can be nicely profitable. Beyond straight profit and extra income, corporations are allowed all sorts of benefits and perks for which the owner pays no taxes.

Take it one step further. If ownership and management of one company are the stepping stones to BMWs and vacations on the Riviera, then the more companies you control through acquisitions, the faster you'll afterburn down the path to true power and luxury. The lesson evident almost daily in the financial news is that it is easier to buy a business than to develop one from the ground up. Not only are the sales and production forces in place, but you can tap the inherent equities in the company you already own as well as the assets of the company you wish to buy. In this way, you reduce the amount of cash you need for the purchase. Or to use that term so popular on the business pages of late—you leverage.

Before going further, let us make some assumptions—about you.

First, you are searching for some avenue by which you can dramatically increase your assets—in other words, get rich.

Two, your experience and goals lie in the business field, not in, say, real estate.

And finally, you are looking for a way to leverage your assets and expand your business interests through acquisition.

The question is how do you get what you want? So far you have probably been frustrated by the fact that companies with good earnings histories are either not for sale or are priced so ridiculously high that only a Fortune 500 megacompany with money to waste could afford them.

This does not mean you have to pack up your checkbook and slink off the playing field. Absolutely not, because there are companies ready to bring in profits for you sitting out there right now. It is merely a question of knowing where to look. And where to look, where these companies are hidden in plain sight, is in this country's bankruptcy courts.

Under the right circumstances, a Chapter 11 company can be purchased on very favorable terms and then turned around, producing an "upside" far beyond that which can be achieved in the stock market.

Bankruptcy courts are federal tribunals usually located in the same building as the federal district courts to which they are subordinate. Unlike district court judges who have a lifetime appointment, bankruptcy judges are appointed for fourteen-year terms. While the quality of those who preside over bankruptcy courts varies throughout the country, overall their quality has been improving in recent years as bankruptcy has become a more central factor in American life, and they have been called upon to supervise business bankruptcy cases of growing size and complexity.

Indeed, the bankruptcy courts of the United States are now administering cases involving more than $60 billion in assets—a rather dubious record. The number of business bankruptcies has steadily risen during the 1980s to about eighty thousand filings annually and involves a major portion of assets being administered in every area of the country. This means there is a huge amount of business assets losing value, being underutilized, and often scrapped—in other words, looking for a "home."

There are two hundred sections to the United States Bankruptcy Code as enacted by Congress and another two hundred rules that were promulgated by the Supreme Court to provide details and procedures to effectuate the sections of the code. These sections are divided into "chapters."

Of most interest here are Chapters 7 and 11. Chapter 7 is concerned with liquidating bankruptcies in which all of the nonexempt assets of the bankruptcy "Debtor" (under the code there are no more "bankrupts") are turned into cash and used to pay the Debtor's debts. Any remaining unpaid debts are then wiped out.

Chapter 11 differs in that it covers a business that seeks protection from creditors' collection activities until a Plan of Reorganization that deals with all the creditors' claims can be proposed. The provisions of Chapter 11 and the related procedural rules provide a framework so that a Debtor may continue to operate its business while under court protection. They also describe how the Debtor may propose and effectuate a Plan of Reorganization.

Chapter 12, new in 1988, gives special protections to family farms, while Chapter 13 allows a wage earner or owner of a very small unincorporated business to reorganize debts through a plan without liquidating nonexempt assets.

Other chapters and corresponding rules are concerned with the organization of the bankruptcy courts; the administration of bankruptcy cases; special bankruptcy rights and duties of the Debtor, creditors, and court officers; and the distributions of "dividends" to creditors.

There is a substantial difference between buying out of Chapter 7 and buying out of Chapter 11. In general, the purpose of purchasing a company out of Chapter 11 is to acquire a complete, operating entity, while Chapter 7 offers an opportunity to purchase assets of a defunct business at deep discount.

Purchasing an operating business offers the best and fastest means for leapfrogging into the executive suite, therefore the focus here will be on Chapter 11 companies. Nonetheless, Chapter 7 is not without its opportunities as well.

A Chapter 7 bankruptcy may result either from a filing of bankruptcy under that chapter of the code or from a conversion of a case filed under Chapter 11 after the company fails to reorganize.

A Chapter 7 proceeding is the death knell of a business, the trustee being, in effect, the undertaker and the probate executor. The trustee's job is to screen claims, liquidate the assets of the estate, and pay the proceeds to creditors in a hierarchy established by the code (after first paying himself his fees and expenses as approved by the bankruptcy judge).

Opportunities to purchase assets of Chapter 7 companies commonly arise in two ways. Assets that appear to have less value than the liens upon them are often turned over to the lienholders and may be bought from them at foreclosure. Assets that have all or a portion of their apparent value free and clear of liens are offered for sale by bankruptcy trustees.

Assets offered at foreclosure or trustee sales are as "distressed" as assets can get. The seller does not follow recognized marketing and management principles for obtaining the best price, but rather, goes for the quickest sale. Usually such assets are sold at auction with only modest public notice to prospective purchasers. As a result, these assets may be purchased at rock-bottom prices—sometimes bordering on a "steal," albeit a legal one.

There is a negative side to Chapter 7 sales. Because the company has ceased to exist, its parts become less than the sum of the former whole. It is very difficult for a buyer to regain any momentum, although it is possible under the right circumstances.

Accordingly, the goal of a Chapter 7 purchase of assets is often either to add onto the purchaser's competing company, or to wheel and deal in the pieces of the former business. In any event, the low prices of the acquired assets allow for options that might not be feasible under other circumstances, opening the way for very large profits.

But the real mother lodes are in Chapter 11 companies. There are approximately sixty thousand cases pending under this chapter in the bankruptcy courts. The vast majority of them involve businesses that continue to operate under court protection from their creditors while attempting to reorganize their finances. Many, many of those companies have valuable assets in products, inventory, goodwill, patents, etc., which are distressed due to undercapitalization or mismanagement, or both.

A large number of companies in Chapter 11 fit a profile identifying them as ripe for purchase. The classic example is a business that has stemmed heavy losses but cannot develop sufficient profits to pay past debts. The owner lacks the resources to reorganize the company and may wish to sell out.

Bankruptcy law has armed the creditors with the power to achieve the sale of the company, over the owner's objection if necessary (only one of the features of bankruptcy law that aid a purchaser). Because the owner and the creditors become frustrated and fearful of the liquidation of the debtor, the price of the company becomes *greatly* discounted.

Enters the prospective purchaser with the turnaround plan. The creditors welcome him as someone who will provide a new beginning and hope for the future. The owner of the troubled company welcomes the chance to bow out of a difficult situation—or faces the prospect of being forced out by the creditors.

If the company holds promise and the price is right, the prospective purchaser offers to buy the company by funding a Plan of Reorganization which provides for payment, usually greatly compromised, to the creditors. The bankruptcy code provides protections for the purchaser that are not available in an out-of-court transaction. If the creditors and the judge approve the plan, the company comes out of Chapter 11 with a new owner, a solid balance sheet, improved goodwill, and opportunity for profit and capital appreciation. At no time has there been a hiatus in operations.

This undoubtedly sounds great in theory. The question then becomes how do you put theory into practice. For that, a knowledge of the bankruptcy process is needed, and that is what this book is all about.

What follows is a step-by-step guide for purchasing a good company out of Chapter 11 . . .

How to discover which companies in your area are in Chapter 11 . . .

How to investigate them . . .

How to determine the best candidates for purchase . . .

How to value their assets and determine their liabilities within the bankruptcy context . . .

Getting to know the major players in most bankruptcy cases and how to negotiate with them . . .

Learning the strategies for acquiring a company AT THE BEST PRICE and taking a company out of Chapter 11 free and clear of its debts.

In addition, there will be a comprehensive and comprehensible explanation of bankruptcy law and practice, which will allow you to master the Chapter 11 process and maneuver within it.

The concepts described will work equally well no matter the size of the company, the nature of the legal entity, or the type of lender.

Once you start applying the precepts laid out in this book, you will be surprised at how little competition you have. Thar's gold in them thar bankruptcy courts and few miners out prospecting in any organized fashion. Company owners are rarely approached by prospective purchasers and the creditors rarely offered an alternative means to achieve some payment upon their claims. Why? Ignorance. Few people know much about the things you will learn from this text.

Before progressing with your education in the field, some groundwork needs to be laid in the form of several more assumptions. One assumption is that you are searching for a small to mid-sized company to purchase, either singly or with one or more partners; next, that such a company is likely to be a corporation owned by one or a few owners and is likely to have a majority of its assets subject to a lien by a business lender, usually a bank. Accordingly, in order to avoid convoluted prose that would make this sound like a Business Law 208 textbook, from now on I will use the terms "the owner" of the "company" (assumed to be a corporation) and "the bank."

Also, some focus must be on you—who and what you are. Success in business is like success in sports. It takes commitment and knowledge as well as innate talents. Whether you are just starting out on your own or whether you already own a business, you need to take an inventory of your personal assets. Do they include the attributes that successful entrepreneurs must have?

Successful entrepreneurs understand that their drive is what powers their businesses. They are willing to spend the extra hours and effort to achieve the rewards. They want to shoulder responsibility and make critical decisions. They have the physical and emotional stamina to do what it takes to get the job done.

The business owner must feel that the rewards are worth the hard work and financial risk required. He should be confident that the rewards, both financial and psychological, exceed what he could achieve elsewhere. He should be pleased that he has escaped being a drudge in the corporate or governmental bureaucracy, and that he has more responsibility. He must be comfortable taking the required financial risks—and be able to sleep at night in spite of them—because he understands what it takes to achieve the riches for which he strives.

Practical experience—expertise—is also needed. Of course, the most promising situation is to take over an existing business in the field in which you have been working. However, many basic business methods are transferable, especially financial concepts and practices. If you will be making a big leap—if you are young and inexperienced or are looking at a business far removed from your area of expertise— you must be confident in your ability to absorb the necessary skills quickly.

There is a way to overcome insufficiencies in your emotional makeup or expertise: make sure the company that you are purchasing has, or will have, people who will complement you. For example, if you are a financial officer, look for a business with a strong sales department. Also, it is always nice to have an experienced and competent production manager. (Of course, good employees in any department are always true assets.) If the company lacks quality in an area in which you are deficient, plan to fill the void with new employees.

One way to insure that you will have the strongest management team is to have a business partner (actually a "shareholder," in the corporate form) whose strengths complement yours. Of course, having a business partner is in many ways like having a marriage partner—wedded life can be blissful or miserable. But keep in mind that most companies in bankruptcy are one-executive businesses where the owner's blind spot has led to trouble. A good partnership greatly increases the chances for success.

In addition to human resources, adequate capital is of utmost importance. *I rank insufficient capital as the number one cause of business bankruptcy filings.* Such a situation leaves no margin for error. Collection or production problems can set off a nasty chain of events. Good opportunities cannot be exploited. Discounts and volume purchasing, which increase profitability, cannot be used. An uptick in bank interest rates can provoke a crisis. The capital-short business is always on the edge of disaster.

Of course, some capital can be borrowed, either based upon personal assets or as part of the refinancing of the company. But you should not delude yourself—unless you can bring fresh capital to a troubled company, you are in great danger of ending up in the same predicament as the previous owner.

On the bright side, less capital is needed to acquire a Chapter 11 company than a profitable business. You get a lot of bang for your buck. Whatever cash and credit you must provide pays off debts and purchases assets at deep discounts. Also, upon a successful reorganization, the balance sheet looks so good that if a modest turnaround can be accomplished, the company will be so attractive to lenders that much or all of the capital you put in can be recouped.

Once even a modest turnabout has been made with your first acquisition, it can then be used both as "credentials" and also a source of capital for additional acquisition, and so on. One word of caution, however. Heading multiple companies requires further honing of management skills and the development of entirely different new ones. The person who wants to climb higher must not neglect his foundation.

That is what you need to put in. Let us not forget what you get out of running a successful business.

First, there is the freedom to do what you think is best, in the manner you think best. No forty-seven layers of corporate, bureaucratic review. No meetings to create compromise proposals for other meetings. Your future will *not* be determined by office politics or people whom you do not even know. If you have conflicts with your boss, it is because you have a split personality!

Second, the profits are yours. A moderately successful business can generate a very handsome income. To a certain extent profits can be retained in the company to provide a cushion in the event of a temporary downtick, sheltered by noncash expense items such as depreciation. A few years of good profits in effect returns the owner's capital contribution, and from then on it is all "free money." No longer will you need to wonder whether the compensation committee will be kind enough to give you a six percent raise.

Good businesses almost automatically build capital appreciation in the form of increasing values in real estate, equipment, accounts receivable, and goodwill (i.e., fairly certain future purchase orders from existing customers). That appreciation can be transformed into bank loans for expansion or acquisition and ultimately may mean a higher price tag on the business should you decide to sell it. Meanwhile, year after year, a portion of the profits can go into pension and profit sharing accounts whose income is tax free.

And then there are the perks. The business operations may "require" a car (insurance, too) paid for by the company. You control the extent and manner of your business entertainment expenses. You decide when to travel to that business meeting or seminar and when to send someone else. You choose the company's health care, pension, and profit-sharing plans. You control your compensation package to mini-mize taxes and maximize fulfilling your needs/wants. There are a million-and-one ways to structure your company's business dealings to provide you with personal, emotional and financial benefits and still keep Uncle Sam happy.

Good business operations lead to good business opportunities. Your dealings with other business people will create a myriad of opportunities, and you do not have to worry that some corporate VP will tell you that the opportunity belongs to your employer and not to you. The credit which your company has built up can form the wherewithal to invest in new ventures.

Moreover, good corporate banking relations lead to good personal banking relations. Your banker calls *you* and asks if there is anything the bank can do for you. Do you want a personal loan for a diamond necklace? Pick up the phone. Do you need investment and estate planning services? Your bank is happy to oblige. The inconveniences of managing money disappear. You become what the bank refers to as a *good* customer. You have what is known as *status*.

Of course, acquiring additional companies multiplies the benefits and adds flexibility. The ability to leverage further acquisitions with the net worth of companies already owned is ridiculously easy. The "track record" opens up additional paths.

Yes, the rewards can be great. That is why, in spite of all the trials and tribulations, every year thousands and thousands of people choose to be their own bosses. But that first step is up to you. Are you ready to handle the quantum leap in power, responsibility, and cash flow?

If you are, the rest is easy.

Chapter 2

The Advantages of Buying an Existing Business

Before going further, let us differentiate between "purchase," and "investment," at least insofar as those terms are used here.

"Purchase" of a business is the acquisition of a sufficient ownership interest to control the operations of the company and the major decisions concerning its future. Obviously, sole ownership in unincorporated or corporate form means total control. If the company is owned through a partnership, the partnership agreement must describe what and how the major partner will control.

Control of a corporation consists of having sufficient voting power of common shares of stock to elect enough directors to control the board of directors and to dictate matters for which shareholder vote is required. In general, control of the board of directors means having enough of the directors committed to acting as requested so that, voting as a block, they can set corporate policy. In a corporation with few stockholders, the shareholders will enter into an agreement that expressly lays out the divisions of power in more detailed ways than the statutes.

"Investment" in a business offers ownership in but not control of a company. In the event of any disagreement when determining a proper course of action, the "other side's" desires will prevail. An investor is betting that the good judgment of the majority holder will produce profits and increase the value of the investment.

Most of the advice in this book concerns the *purchase* of a business, rather than investment. It is directed toward the reader who wants to be his own boss, who wants to make his own mistakes, and who wants to control the corporate purse strings. Besides, most people who turn around bankrupt companies believe that past management was a major cause of the problem and prefer to have them removed from any decision-making capacity.

However, no slight is intended toward the investor. Investing in turning around a business is more exciting than owning real estate and more "hands on" than playing the stock market. In fact, it can lead to far more dramatic, ongoing profits than can be achieved in the stock market. It is a way to take part in operating a business while not devoting full time and talent to it.

In any event, while the text is directed toward the takeover, take-charge type, the concepts presented here work equally well for an investor. The investor must still know how to locate the bankrupt companies, investigate them, and lead a company out of bankruptcy. He must know how to deal with the parties to the bankruptcy case and how to get the best possible deal. The only difference is that he will be relying upon the continuing efforts of the present owner to provide the "laboring oar" of the reorganization process.

Because the present owner of the company will be retained, the most important aspect of investing is to have the right fit between the holdover owner and the investor. The investor must be confident that the problems of the business cannot be traced to extremely poor management or fraud by the owner; rather, that the owner was and is an asset to the business. The investor must feel that the existing team needs only the addition of the investor's capital and, perhaps, a little of the investor's advice, to move to profitability.

Sometimes the talents of the present owner are not considered initially by the prospective buyer, but become evident as the investigation of the company proceeds. Thus the prospective purchaser who storms onto the scene bent on an all-or-nothing takeover may find that he wants the present owner to continue as an executive and minority or majority shareholder. Consequently, for philosophical reasons (as well as for some tactical reasons, discussed in later chapters), the prospective buyer should maintain an open mind as to whether purchase of an entire, a majority, or a minority ownership interest will be a profitable course of action.

Starting a new business from the ground up is a luxury few can afford. The essential problem is that a great deal of money and time must be expended before the first sale is made, much less the first dollar taken in. It is very difficult to acquire substantial bank loans at an early stage for what institutional lenders consider to be venture capital.

An organization must be created from whole cloth. Much time must be expended searching for and interviewing prospective employees. Relationships with suppliers and customers must be developed rapidly.

The usual traumas of finding suitable premises—the seemingly endless hours of walk-throughs and learning the subtle deficiencies of the sites and the one-upmanship strategies of the landlords—is magnified for the start-up owner. There are other important, time-consuming things that also have to be done at the same time. The premises must be viewed, and lease terms negotiated, without knowing just how production and finances will be organized in six months or a year. For example, do you aim for a relatively short-term lease and plan to move soon, or do you secure better terms but lock yourself in by negotiating a long term?

In summary, the start-up owner is required to spread himself very thin at the initiation of the enterprise and to "reinvent the wheel" for just about every facet of the business.

By contrast, even a business that is not running very well has a hundred aspects that are progressing at least tolerably and do not require much attention from the owner. Quite possibly, adjustments can and should be made in those elements over time, to improve productivity, save money, and/or keep up with changing times, but the business will not stand or fall on those items' deficiencies.

By definition, the operating business is settled in its premises and has an organization that sells the product and gets it out the door. Employees are at their work stations regularly, and procedures are already in place to respond to minor glitches and major crises. Most workers have a reasonably good idea of acceptable techniques and logistics. Each component function of the operations is manned by someone who is responsible for it.

As proof of the benefits of an existing organization, take a look around where you are presently employed. Isolate the separate functions. Note the line of command, and how that relates to the manner in which the employees are physically deployed. Note the manner in which the employees are informed of internal and external matters. Become sensitized as to how the organization acquires its lowly office supplies, keeps track of them, and distributes them. Consider the complexity of the rules respecting health coverage, absences, vacations, and proper conduct. List the unwritten rules of the company "culture" which nevertheless everyone knows to follow. Review the written materials that describe rules of conduct and organizational matters. Developing all those facets took many decisions and much, much time.

(Seen in this context, a franchise is a compromise. It is a start-up situation, but the nature of the operations fits a standardized pattern, and so the franchisor is able to make many of the necessary financial and operational decisions. Also, ideally, the franchisor has already created the customer goodwill.)

Of course, a major benefit of the existing business is that it is producing income *right now*. Maybe not as much as you would like, maybe not as much as it will after you take over, but still it is there. (The business with the most potential will be operating at or near a break-even level.) It has an established customer base, not just projections of future customers. It has a network of regular suppliers that helps the company produce the product that brings in the income.

The point is not that you must find an established business without problems—there are none—but that if you purchase such an entity, even a troubled company, it will have specific, *known* problems upon which you can *concentrate your efforts* in the context of an *existing operational framework*.

Strangely enough, suppliers are easier to deal with when you owe them money than at the outset of the relationship. First, they recall the profits they have made on past sales. Second, it is always easier to continue sales to a customer than to seek out and establish new customers. Third, they would rather not burn their bridges either by giving a customer an excuse to withhold payment or by taking action that forces the customer into litigation. In short, the creditors of a troubled business actually have vested financial and psychological interests in maintaining the continued existence of the troubled debtor and are often more cooperative than would be imagined.

Such a situation is in contrast to the difficulty a new company has in establishing its credit with suppliers. In a start-up situation, the creditors are hanging back until they see your dollar already at work, the sales made, and the product out the door...that is, until you have already "bootstrapped" yourself into the ranks of the established businesses. Thus the purchaser of an established business gets far more leverage out of his dollars because of the creditors' unintentional investment in the business.

Of course, often the troubled business has expended its goodwill, which must be rebuilt. However, to borrow an advertising maxim, negative name recognition can be better than no recognition at all. In any event, the appearance of new ownership on the scene instantaneously wipes out the bad will, at least for a "honeymoon" period. The suppliers' and customers' psychological investment in the company is usually that strong.

Consequently, while starting "from scratch" has certain advantages for management, purchase of an existing business at a reasonable price provides far more for the investment dollar and provides a better framework for the allocation of executives' time and energies.

A basic concept of real estate investment is that of "leveraging"— that is, putting as little up-front hard cash into the purchase as possible by borrowing a large portion of the purchase price. Most families, for example, put down no more than twenty percent of the price of their homes, paying for the rest with a mortgage loan. The same technique commonly is being used for corporate acquisitions. In fact, the complexity of an operating business provides a greater range of leveraging possibilities than does real estate, and the acquisition of a bankrupt company adds a few more dimensions.

It is common to borrow a portion of the purchase price of a business. There are many sources of collateral in the company, such as machinery and equipment, inventory, and accounts receivable. The availability of different types of collateral allows the prospective borrower more leeway to persuade the possible lender of the solid value of the individual classes of assets than can be done with real estate, which is generally appraised as one asset. If the purchaser already owns a successful business, not only may specific assets of his company serve as collateral for the acquisition loan, but its general net worth also serves to provide an additional guarantee.

Acquisition of a company operating under bankruptcy protection offers certain additional forms of leveraging. Although it stretches the term "leveraging" a bit, buying at the heavy discount available through the bankruptcy court buys for a dollar what the former owner and the creditors may have paid ten dollars to build. Also, as more fully discussed later, the bankrupt company's lender wants the company to survive to avoid taking a loss, so the lender may be a ready-made source for future loans.

Successful leveraging can easily lead to pyramiding. Once an acquisition has been made, if new management can cause revenues and/or profits to start a climb, it is not too difficult to persuade a lender that the acquired company provides collateral towards the next acquisition. How much one wishes to subject past acquisitions to the liabilities of new acquisitions is a matter of personal style, but there is no doubt that they can form a base to allow for the acquisition of ever bigger and better companies. (An alternative is to sell companies purchased earlier and turned around, and to utilize the profits from the sales of those companies to acquire new businesses.)

Leveraging and pyramiding have their risks, as the intertwining of liabilities can lead to a domino effect that damages all units in the structure. However, a lesson in this era of conglomerates and megacorporations is that, if the owner has the talent to maintain control over his empire, having more entities and more complex interrelationships between them provides more room to maneuver and therefore less chance of collapse than might be expected.

Many good companies for sale are not advertised to the public, whether they are in or out of bankruptcy. However, much information about companies operating under bankruptcy court protection is in public records, and so a format can be developed for ferreting them out.

It is generally difficult to locate companies outside bankruptcy and to approach owners. Even if the owners might otherwise be interested in selling, unsolicited overtures are usually met with suspicion. The majority of regular business brokers do not usually have access to the better businesses, mostly concentrating on bars and restaurants. Finding a profitable company for sale at the right time is mostly a matter of personal connections or luck.

The owner of a profitable company who will entertain suitors is doing so for one of two reasons: either he is hoping to extract a premium price, or the business has hidden problems and is not really profitable or is imminently about to become unprofitable. It is very difficult to locate profitable companies for sale at a reasonable price. Companies that have already been forced to disclose their problems and that are seeking help are preferable.

It is the rare company in Chapter 11 that is not, in effect, for sale. Many owners are actively seeking investors or purchasers, whether totally voluntarily or as a result of pressures from creditors or the court. Even unsolicited interest from outsiders is rarely turned aside. The owner needs solutions, and frequently those solutions are outside his capabilities. If the owner is uncooperative, procedures exist in bankruptcy to bypass the owner and force the sale of the company with the cooperation of the creditors.

So where are those "For Sale" signs? They are the "petitions" that commence the Chapter 11 cases. They are, figuratively, hanging on the court file jackets and stamped on the pleadings in the files. It is merely a matter of knowing how to find them.

PART II

BUYING OUT OF CHAPTER 11

Chapter 3

Why You Should Assay Chapter 11 Companies (Or, Thar's Gold in Them Thar Halls)

After the Great Crash of 1929, businessmen jumped out of windows rather than file bankruptcy. Times have changed. Today, the business owner who seemingly has reached the end of the rope reaches for the federal lifeline—bankruptcy court protection.

In today's culture, it is considered legitimate to use the legal system to hold off creditors in order to save an owner's interests. In general, our society has become more fluid and less rigid than it once was. It is easier and more acceptable to establish new relationships of all types. That holds true in business, where there is now less loyalty and "honor." Today, rarely does a business owner follow what once would have been considered the "honorable" path.

Beyond that, the legal system has made bankruptcy a more viable and palatable alternative than it once was. A sweeping revision of the federal bankruptcy laws, which went into effect in October, 1979, realigned debtor-creditor interests across the country. (There are no state bankruptcy laws—they were entirely preempted by federal statutes in the early 1800s.) Because the last prior major revision was in 1898, the drafters of the new bankruptcy code tossed out many established concepts and attempted to restructure the bankruptcy process to reflect modern economic realities. Some feel that the drafters ended up creating a whole new reality inside the bankruptcy court which is more debtor-oriented than the actual financial and commercial climate of the outside world.

Without going into a detailed discussion of the bankruptcy code, it will suffice to say that the new code took a lot of arrows out of the creditors' quivers. Before the revisions, for example, secured creditors were able to repossess their collateral easily. Now, however, even if the Debtor's business is in default, it can, in most cases, hang on to and use that collateral during the Chapter 11 proceedings, as long as the secured creditor's interests are "protected." (This is a bankruptcy term of art that means that the collateral is not diminishing in value.)

Another key change in the code was to remove any suggestion from the laws that a trustee can be appointed to operate a Chapter 11 company unless it can be shown that the Debtor demonstrated extreme mismanagement or fraud. The result is that, while a few bones are thrown to the creditors, the Debtor, in most cases, remains at the reins of the troubled company.

One other factor should not be overlooked. Our attitudes about bankruptcy have changed because there are so many more bankruptcies. This is a result of the complexity and changeability of our economy, forcing more companies into the "troubled" category, thus providing more grist for the bankruptcy mill.

And so in the 1980s, we saw an increasing number of large, public companies availing themselves of the protection of the bankruptcy courts, whether as a defensive measure to fend off creditors accumulated through overexpansion (e.g., Wickes), product liability suits (e.g., Johns-Manville, A. H. Robins), other errors (e.g., Texaco), or as an offensive weapon to break union contracts (e.g., Continental Airlines). In each case the loss of public confidence resulting from the filing of the Chapter 11 petition was deemed to be a reasonable price to pay for the restructuring of the company's circumstances which could be accomplished through the invoking of the bankruptcy code.

Many, many smaller and not-so-famous companies have also chosen the same route. The statistics tell the story. During the last ten years, the rate of Chapter 11 bankruptcy filings has steadily climbed, from 3,266 in 1978, to 14,059 in 1982, to 24,740 in 1986. At this time there are approximately sixty thousand Chapter 11 cases pending.

The average length of Chapter 11 cases also continues to grow, with a large number of companies operating under bankruptcy court supervision for more than a year, with their prebankruptcy debts frozen. The judges, often with the concurrence of the creditors, allow the companies to maintain the status quo for so long because they are more valuable as ongoing businesses than as piecemeal assets, and they have the potential to become profitable again. However, most lack the resources to rehabilitate themselves, and so they eventually decline and are liquidated.

Thus, although the bankruptcy law encourages increasing numbers of Chapter 11 cases, the process does not really help most businesses to reorganize. The main reason for such an unsatisfactory ending to those cases and companies is that Chapter 11 often exacerbates the major problem facing troubled businesses—insufficient capital. Many companies file bankruptcy petitions because of insufficient capital, but once under court protection they discover the hard realities of Chapter 11: banks will not lend to them, and business brokers will not list them. Of course, many of them also lack management of the caliber necessary to produce profits.

While there is no precise moment to approach a company in Chapter 11, it is when the company gets mired in the bankruptcy process that owners get desperate to raise capital or sell out, and creditors start looking for any way to move the case off dead center. Thus, companies that have been in bankruptcy for nine months or more are often easily put into "play" by a potential investor or purchaser. As the time in bankruptcy grows past a year, commonly all of the involved parties become quite anxious to find an "angel."

The opportunities are there. The key is knowing how to find them, maneuver through the process, and negotiate a good deal for the purchase.

It is not that difficult to learn how to play the game. While it is true that the bankruptcy process is an arcane area of law, it is not that difficult to learn enough to become a winning player. (Of course, at the final stages, an experienced attorney should be used.) This book will provide you with sufficient instruction to earn your degree in Buying Out of Bankruptcy. You will then be ready to apply what you have learned to the real world.

Businesses file Chapter 11 proceedings because they have something to save.

The typical Chapter 11 company is maintaining ordinary operations at the time it files its bankruptcy petition and continues to do so after filing. The product is going out the door, and sales are being made. The equipment is operating, and the employees are on the job, on a daily schedule. The inventory, equipment, machinery, and real estate have substantial value, which is protected and even enhanced by being kept in use. Companies that have ceased operations or that are on an accelerating downward course usually just close their doors or file for liquidation under Chapter 7.

One reason why companies' operations change very little or not at all due to the filing of the Chapter 11 is that bankruptcy law and practice heavily favor a Chapter 11 company operating through its executives as "Debtor in Possession" rather than through a court-appointed trustee. The officers and directors automatically retain their management authority upon the filing of the case unless, as already mentioned, a creditor can show fraud or gross conduct. The reason for this is the creators and the practitioners of the bankruptcy laws continue to believe that, whatever problems a Chapter 11 company has, its circumstances are usually harmed severely by replacing management with a trustee. (See a more complete discussion of Chapter 11 trusteeships in Chapter 4.)

The "Debtor in Possession" retains ownership and control over its assets and can enter into contracts, buy supplies, and sell its products in the ordinary course of its business without prior court approval. Its daily operations are under the control of its management, and it is not uncommon for most procedures to be unchanged. After the initial shock of the bankruptcy filing has worn off, most employees virtually forget that the company is a Chapter 11 Debtor. (While technically in most cases the Debtor will be operating under Chapter 11 as a "Debtor in Possession," for convenience a Chapter 11 company will be referred to here merely as "the Debtor.")

Certain results of filing Chapter 11 actually enhance the company's operations, the major boost being the freezing of unsecured and tax debts that arose prior to the filing. The bankruptcy law prohibits the Debtor from making *any* payments to those creditors unless and until it files an overall Plan of Reorganization. Thus management can turn away from the time-consuming process of stiffing the creditors piecemeal! Also, since the company does not have to devote any portion of receipts to old debt until a plan is approved, present operations in effect get a cash infusion.

Another tactic that can give a Chapter 11 company a boost is simply planning ahead. Often the executives foresee the Chapter 11 some months before it is necessary to file the case. Consequently, during those months they can see to it that there is a steady increase in the accounts payable. The result is that the company has a nice cushion of inventory and supplies—and, frequently, cash in the bank—on the date the petition is filed. In bankruptcy parlance, the company has acquired a "war chest."

The Chapter 11 filing may add to problems with suppliers if they refuse to sell or require cash payment on delivery; however, with proper massaging most suppliers come around. The Debtor in Possession's most effective argument to suppliers is that they are *better off* selling on credit during the Chapter 11 than they were selling to an insolvent company prior to the filing, because bankruptcy law requires the Debtor in Possession to keep the company's payment's current.

Usually the laws of supply and demand also work to insure that the suppliers will not put the Chapter 11 company out of business. Often the Debtor can successfully remind the major suppliers that helping the Debtor stay in business increases the chances for payment on the prior debt and for future sales. If that argument fails, in most industries there are alternative suppliers who are hungry for business.

Chapter 11 companies rarely have serious problems with the creditors in the bankruptcy proceedings during the months following the initiation of the case. The bankruptcy does not change the fact that creditors are always two steps (at least) behind in the creditor-debtor chase. Few creditors appear for the initial meeting when the Debtor is required to answer questions about its assets, liabilities, history, and operations. Those that do usually limit their inquiry to "When do I get paid?" Although the Debtor, in theory, is subject to questioning at other times, creditors hardly ever take advantage of their rights to delve into the Chapter 11 company's circumstances. Rarely does a creditor investigate the Debtor's financial records in detail. As a result, the creditors do not really know or understand the Chapter 11 company's operations and remain powerless to significantly affect them.

The judge is not really a fearsome overseer. In fact, rather than being the all-seeing eye, *by law* the judge is *prohibited* from reviewing the disclosures filed by the Debtor or inquiring into its operations on his own initiative. The theory is that a bankruptcy judge is not an administrator, but rather an adjudicator limited to the specific judicial function of deciding disputes among the parties.

The judge remains in the dark about the Chapter 11 company unless and until someone places a specific dispute before him, initiated by formal complaint or motion. If the dispute arises from a creditor who wishes to install a trustee or convert the case to a Chapter 7 liquidation, the judge may learn a good deal about the company during the course of the adversarial process. If the dispute is over the amount of one creditor's claim, the judge may learn little about the Debtor. Sometimes, like the blind man feeling the elephant's trunk and calling the animal skinny, the judge may acquire a distorted view of the Debtor.

In many cases, the only party that keeps something of an eye on the debtor is the United States Trustee. The U.S. Trustee is charged with leading the questioning of the Debtor at the initial meeting of creditors and seeing to it that the Debtor files the required disclosures and reports and otherwise follows the Chapter 11 rules. However, for policy reasons, the U.S. Trustee is not an active or aggressive player in Chapter 11 cases, and the office is overburdened. So except for the more egregious circumstances, the U.S. Trustee does not affect Chapter 11 operations.

The point of all this is not that Chapter 11 businesses are trouble free, but rather that the filing of the case usually does not make the situation worse, and often actually helps. The Chapter 11 company is not greatly impeded in its operations. The creditors are relegated to the background. As a result, the momentum, or, if you will, the inertia, passes to the Chapter 11 Debtor. So Chapter 11 of the bankruptcy code clearly does serve one of its intended purposes—allowing a troubled company a breather from its creditors.

The result is that companies frequently stabilize their operations while in Chapter 11. There is a period of relative calm during which management can concentrate on operations and many companies move to at least a "break-even" status. Management of some companies then take the opportunity to attack the underlying problems and set the stage for a turnaround. Other D.I.P.'s become quite dependent on the temporary and false "drug" of court protection, and make few changes. Either way, the business is preserved and often improved, at least in the short run.

Because of the sometimes surprising dynamics of Chapter 11, you are not likely to find the field littered with the corporate equivalent of "played-out" mines but rather with active, operating businesses. Those companies will have substantial and useful assets, tangible and intangible—the "gold" that still remains available to the astute prospector, albeit somewhat hidden and covered with "dirt." This book will show you how to determine which companies merit further investigation and how to purchase them at the best possible price.

There are companies in bankruptcy that can become profitable for you. Many businesses are not inherently losers. They have specific problems that can be attacked.

But let us not minimize the problems or risks. The reality of a troubled company is a wealth of unpleasant details and negative trends. Your initial investigation into the business will probably disclose a discouraging financial history, disorganization, missed opportunities, etc.

But do not lose heart. Alongside the dross will be some pebbles that glint through the layers of muck, some ore that, you would swear, if it just could be cleaned, might prove to be gold. Among the many businesses in Chapter 11 that probably should be laid to rest, you will find a few that you would swear could become profitable if only you could get your hands on them.

Perhaps you will find a situation where your skills, experience, temperament, and/or capital will supply the missing pieces of the puzzle the present owner has been unable to solve. You can see that the company has a basically good product and that sales could be increased. You can see how production can be made more efficient, how costs can be cut. You can see how additional capital can cure many chronic problems. You realize that if the past debt can be cleared up at a reasonable price, you soon could be in the president's chair of a gold mine. When all the pieces come together they will spell "profit."

But, is it worth it to jump into a bankruptcy situation? What if the owner does not want to sell?

Many Chapter 11 companies are for sale.

Many owners welcome prospective purchasers. Some are frustrated at their inability to gain profitability, others simply are "burned out." Many hope that the fresh capital will arrive in the form of an investor who will retain them as partners. There are owners, especially older ones, who realize that they lack the stamina and/or the will to do what has to be done to accomplish a turnaround.

Shakespeare once noted about war that "The better part of valor is discretion." The same holds true for an owner struggling against bankruptcy. He, no doubt, has guaranteed the bank loan and would have to pay any deficiency or file a Chapter 7 bankruptcy himself in the event of liquidation of the business. If he has failed to pay the "trust" portion of his employees' withholding and social security taxes to the government, he is personally liable, on a debt that is not dischargeable in personal bankruptcy. (To all officers of troubled companies: DO NOT FAIL TO PAY "TRUST" TAXES TO THE GOVERNMENT!)

Many owners would rather not sell, but are coerced by the creditors. The creditors already may be pursuing the owner to "do something" when you arrive on the scene. In any event, the appearance of a potential purchaser at once will increase the creditors' pressure on the owner substantially. In many cases, it is this high pressure which produces quick sales of companies at very reasonable prices, as the creditors do not want to hear any more of the owner's excuses, or pie-in-the-sky, or—anything except the end of the Chapter 11 case.

One unique feature of Chapter 11 is that creditors can go beyond mere complaining and force the sale of the company over the owner's objection. With certain limitations, discussed more fully later, a creditor may propose a Plan of Reorganization which is funded by sale of the company, and, if the other creditors approve, the court may order such sale *over the objection of the owner.* Those bankruptcy provisions, which give new meaning to the term "unwanted takeover," create powerful incentives for the owner to come face-to-face with cold, hard reality and negotiate a sale of the company himself. If not, reality may get him from behind.

Whatever the mix of reasons, only a minority of owners will absolutely refuse to talk with a potential "angel" or will not consider selling.

If a company is operating at or near "break even" during the Chapter 11, it will not be closed down by the bankruptcy court too soon. Those creditors who began the case with optimism begin to wilt; the pessimists write off the debt totally. After about six months, just about every credit manager has put the file into the cabinet and has gone on to more immediate problems. After that, anything that comes in a dividend from the court is "found money."

Because the creditors' momentum is stopped, they are always over-joyed to see a possible purchaser or investor appear on the scene. It is not hard for an outsider to work with them. They are *easy* to work with. They are ready to accept a fraction of their claims as payment in full.

If the unsecured creditors are discouraged enough, they may accept the equivalent of nothing. It is not unusual for the unsecured creditors to accept, say, ten percent on their claims payable over three years—which, after accounting for inflation, is practically nothing. In extreme cases, creditors will accept installment payments conditioned on future *profits* of the Chapter 11 company. Sometimes they will accept stock—in a company which has a negative net worth!

(Thus the bankruptcy has served yet another purpose for the Debtor: with very little effort it has turned a bunch of bothersome, steel-hard creditors into malleable suppliants who can be dealt with *en masse*.)

In most business cases there is one major secured creditor, usually a lender, usually a bank. The bank often has a blanket lien on all of the Debtor's assets, which quite possibly will not pay the full amount of the bank's claim upon a liquidation. So, while the bank's lawyer "struts and frets his hour upon the stage," bluffing that the bank wants to be handed the keys to the company, really the bank wants nothing more than to see the company find its way out of its problems.

In fact, the banker prays for reorganization twice as hard as the trade creditors because bankers are hired, paid, and retained as bankers for making *good* loans. His boss does not like to put loans on the "nonperforming" list to which the federal regulators pay special attention. His boss likes even less to write off the loans entirely. The banker wants to return the loan to the "good" category, and so he is looking for any excuse to rewrite it.

The best excuse for the banker to paper over the mistake is "new ownership." A new face allows for new positive assumptions. It replaces a relationship between the banker and the prior owner gone sour, and so has elements of a new loan. It pushes the day of reckoning on the original loan into the distant future, and may even avoid that reckoning altogether. Therefore, the banker has more psychological reasons to rewrite the loan than he originally did to write it!

Because of the incentives to the banker, it is not uncommon for him to be soft on loan terms. He may extend the period to pay back the loan, and/or lower the amount of the installment payments. Sometimes he will even lend fresh money to a new owner. He will do anything to paper over the bad loan.

Sometimes the Debtor will have defenses to major creditors' claims, or it will have counterclaims, and often those creditors are willing to compromise their claims further to avoid litigation. For example, in today's legal climate banks are especially afraid of being found liable for their usual heavy-handed tactics prior to the bankruptcy. If the unsecured creditor is looking ahead to a likely small dividend upon its claim, it may not be economically feasible to incur substantial litigation expenses.

Another factor which depresses the purchase price of a Chapter 11 company is that the assets become undervalued. Perhaps devaluation is justified, as the assets are not producing profits. However, usually the creditors go further, and mentally write off goodwill and patents, and write down accounts receivable, machinery, and inventory, whether or not justified. The smart shopper will see that the tangibles and intangibles will have greater value in his hands.

An inescapable fact of life for the owner is that his company has a "negative net worth," or, put another way, the "Shareholder's Equity" line item on the balance sheet is a negative number. In effect, the creditors really have made a greater investment in the company than the owner. The creditors, being asked to accept cents on the dollar, are in no mood to allow the owner to receive a substantial portion of the purchase price, and the bankruptcy laws back them up. (See discussion of hierarchy of debt, in Chapter 7.) As a result, the buyer does not have to chisel the owner—the creditors will do it for him—and the owner often walks away with little or nothing for his interest in the company.

The natural outcome of this is that all parties often welcome an inquiry from a potential purchaser, and then find themselves in no position to refuse the most modest—insulting, even—offer for the company.

It is surprising how few people are searching to uncover the opportunities that exist in bankruptcy court. While there may be good reasons for the paucity of prospectors, those reasons do not detract from the validity of the concepts presented here—and in fact they *reinforce* them.

The major reason is that very few people know how to go about searching for, investigating, and proposing the purchase of a Chapter 11 company. Without adequate advice, the bankruptcy process is baffling. Without an educated overview, the interests and desires of the numerous parties are hard to place.

Another reason for the failure of outsider interest in Chapter 11 companies is the fear on the part of those not already associated with the Debtor that any overtures will be met with derision. Nothing could be further from the truth. Parties often are crying out for outside help, but are normally too paralyzed by the Chapter 11 battles to market the company. Most of the time, neither the owner nor the creditors know how to find investors or purchasers. Even when doing "cold calls" to Chapter 11 companies, feelers of possible purchasers almost never are rejected out of hand.

The organized search for Chapter 11 "gold" simply is a situation waiting to happen. The first prospectors are just noticing the "flecks" on the "ground." People are just awakening to the large number of opportunities that are available. In the "gold rush" which is just beginning, the quick will reap the early and best rewards. In the process, bankruptcy court will never be the same again, much like takeovers in the 1980s irrevocably affected the stock market.

The whole purpose of purchasing a Chapter 11 company is to pay so little that you are convinced that you cannot lose. The counterbalance for the added risk of buying a troubled company is the lessened sums which you place at risk. You may buy the company at little more than the amount the assets would bring if you fail and have to liquidate. (Of course, there is always Chapter 11!) You may have minimal personal exposure.

(This brings us to an irony of the bankruptcy law: in forgiving their claims for a pittance, the trade creditors will in effect have invested more in the company than its legal owner.)

Because of the relatively low investment, a modest turnaround can produce a handsome return. The new owner often will take out in compensation an amount in the first year or two which will, as a practical matter, return the original capital contribution to him. Another variation is to show the uptick in sales to a banker and have the company borrow money that is then used to fund, among other things, the return of a good deal of the new owner's capital contribution. The result: within a short time, the new owner may have little money at risk, and so his return on capital approaches "infinite."

Besides limiting his risk, the owner will have opened up opportunities. The return of his capital, and his return on capital, provide funds for expansion or other investments. The improving sales and profits—not to mention the balance sheet made beautiful upon the emergence from Chapter 11—open new opportunities for borrowing.

You should not forget what is perhaps the ultimate measure of success. If the turnaround is very successful, the owner acquires the option of selling the company at the premium price that a profitable company demands.

Buying any business is tricky, and dealing with a company that is in bankruptcy adds another dimension, but this book will help you to be prepared. Have confidence to take that leap. Have confidence that you have enough experience in the business world to manage a company. Be ready to improve your circumstances. When you feel you are ready, you are!

There has to be a first time for everything. J.P. Morgan had to do his first deal. Andrew Carnegie had to own his first corporation. Once you have bought your first company out of bankruptcy, you will be back for more.

It is not that hard. After you have closed your first purchase, you will wonder why it took you so long to take the plunge.

Chapter 4

The Chapter 11 Process

Even though the bankruptcy code tilts the playing field a little in the Debtor's favor, filing a Chapter 11 case is usually not high on a chief executive's list of preferred options. However, when existence outside of bankruptcy court protection becomes untenable due to creditor actions, often a Chapter 11 proceeding offers the only chance to save the company.

Consequently, it is only when the owner and executives have a strong will to overcome adversity that a company will be placed into Chapter 11. The principals of the company believe that there is something worth saving and are committed to putting forth substantial efforts to that end. Businesses that are hopelessly unprofitable will simply be allowed to die.

In nearly all the cases, the company is operating at the onset of the bankruptcy, and it is essential that it continue to operate while in Chapter 11. The bankruptcy code favors that course of action as the best means to rehabilitate businesses, and so most companies have a fighting chance to hold their place in the market while they attack financial problems. Many companies are able to achieve the goal of having the daily work environment of the production and office employees virtually unaffected by the existence of the bankruptcy case, thus maintaining morale.

Of course, the ultimate goal of the Debtor is to use the period of the Chapter 11 case to correct the problems that caused the filing, recapitalize, and propose payment to the creditors. The proposal is made in the form of a Plan of Reorganization, which must lay out a coordinated scheme to pay all creditors, consistent with the hierarchy of creditors and other requirements established by the bankruptcy code and rules.

Once the creditors and the court have approved the plan, the company will emerge from the shadows of bankruptcy into the sunlight of the free market without any hiatus in operations. The balance sheet will be much improved after compromising the creditors' claims through the plan, and the company will be in a good posture to become profitable again.

For many companies those goals are realistic, for many others they are not. Chapter 11 will provide the crucible.

Any person or entity may file a bankruptcy "petition," which is nothing more than a one-page declaration that the party wishes to invoke the protection of the bankruptcy laws. The petition is filed with the clerk of the bankruptcy court in the federal district in which the individual debtor resides or the business entity has its home office. Upon the filing of the voluntary petition, a case number is designated, a court file is opened, and the case is assigned to a bankruptcy judge. The debtor becomes a Debtor.

A person or company may be forced into an unwanted bankruptcy if three creditors holding a total of at least five thousand dollars in claims together file an "involuntary" petition. The Debtor may choose the "chapter"—that is whether it wishes to reorganize or be liquidated. If the person or company does not concede to the validity of the bankruptcy, a hearing is held within a few weeks of the filing of the petition at which the bankruptcy judge determines whether the proposed Debtor is "insolvent" according to bankruptcy code standards. If so, the bankruptcy case is commenced, the Debtor chooses a "chapter," and the Debtor is placed under court supervision just as if the case had been filed voluntarily.

At the moment that a Chapter 11 bankruptcy petition is filed, the claims against the Debtor are "frozen." The Debtor cannot pay those debts until it proposes a Plan of Reorganization to deal with all of them, and the creditors cannot continue with any collection activities. While the secured creditors (e.g., banks, equipment vendors) generally cannot demand return of their collateral at the onset of the case, the Debtor must nevertheless reach some accommodation with them that allows the Debtor to use the collateral in its Chapter 11 operations, usually in return for monthly payments. The Debtor must, in the ordinary course, pay all of its operating obligations that arise *after* the filing of the petition and are thus considered "costs of administration" of the bankruptcy case.

When a bankruptcy case is initiated, the Debtor must file a statement covering all assets and liabilities, on a form entitled "Schedules of Assets and Liabilities" which is uniform throughout the United States. If the Debtor is operating, or has operated, a business, a "Statement of Financial Affairs for Debtor Engaged in Business" form must also be filed. The forms are referred to commonly as "the Schedules." (They are reproduced in Appendices A and B.) If the Schedules are not filed at the same time as the petition, they are to be filed within fifteen days thereafter, although it is not unusual for the court to grant an extension.

Between twenty and forty days after the filing of the voluntary petition or the court's finding that the involuntary party is to be deemed a Debtor, a meeting of creditors is held. The meeting is scheduled by the United States Trustee and is usually held at the Trustee's office. Notice of the meeting is sent to all creditors, and they may attend and ask questions of the Debtor relating to the bankruptcy case. The assistant U.S. Trustee presiding over the meeting leads off by going through a checklist of questions, including verifying insurance coverage. (If the case is a Chapter 7, the meeting is presided over by a trustee—usually a bankruptcy attorney in private practice—who is appointed by the U.S. Trustee.) In many business cases, the meeting is continued to one or more later dates to provide sufficient time for creditors to formulate questions, investigate the operations of the Debtor, and follow up on matters raised at the initial meeting.

While the creditors' meeting provides a forum for questioning the Debtor, it is by no means the creditors' only opportunity to get answers to questions or financial information from the Debtor. Generally speaking, any creditor or other party in interest may investigate any aspect of the Debtor's past or present operations, finances, and transactions. Most bankruptcy attorneys acknowledge this reality, and so creditors usually can obtain answers to questions, review of books and records, or inspection of premises, for the asking. In cases of lack of cooperation, the party may request the court to order an employee of the Debtor to sit for an examination with a court reporter present. The party may also ask that the Debtor produce documents, etc. The Debtor is also required to file operating reports with the Clerk of Court and the U.S. Trustee.

Now let us look at business operations under Chapter 11.

The bankruptcy laws lean toward reorganizing businesses rather than liquidating them. That is why if creditors band together to file an "involuntary" bankruptcy under Chapter 7 against a business, the Debtor may convert the case to that under Chapter 11. Also, the law provides that the management of a Chapter 11 debtor ordinarily continues to operate the company as a Debtor in Possession.

Rarely is a Chapter 11 trustee appointed to run the business. It is inherently damaging to drop an outsider into the chief operating officer's place. Even worse, the trustee usually is a practicing bankruptcy attorney, not an experienced business executive. Since the mandate of the Chapter 11 trustee is to maintain the status quo, such a manager cannot be expected to take any major steps to improving the company's operations. This is why bankruptcy judges will appoint Chapter 11 trustees only if management has engaged in serious fraud or *gross* mismanagement. (The existence of a Chapter 11 trustee in a case should be a "red flag" for an investor. On one hand it indicates severe management problems. On the other hand it probably means a situation where the court and the creditors are anxious to put the company into new hands.)

In the vast majority of cases, a company that has filed a Chapter 11 petition simply continues with its ordinary operations. In terms of the everyday humdrum, no one would notice a change. Decisions within the ordinary course of the workday are made by management in the same manner as they were before the petition was filed. Although the business is under the theoretical supervision of the bankruptcy court, no court personnel observe operations or watch over the books and records. While the U.S. Trustee reviews the operating reports and occasionally takes action if the Debtor crosses certain "trip wires," the U.S. Trustee's supervision of the Debtor is normally nonintrusive and passive.

Extra-ordinary (sic) actions can be taken—"outside the ordinary course of business"—if prior court approval is first acquired. A Chapter 11 company then can borrow additional money and further encumber its property, buy and finance expensive machinery, sign leases for additional space, prosecute lawsuits, or hire top executives or consultants. This leads to an irony: the bankruptcy judge—a nonowner, nonoperator—gets the final say in the exercise of business judgment.

Of course, life is not all wine and roses for the owner of a Chapter 11 company. The creditors can stick their noses into the company's business and can try to skew decisions to help their own interests. Management prerogatives certainly are narrowed. But all in all, the bankruptcy law does not require a wrenching change in the mode of operations. (Thus a major irony of the bankruptcy system is produced: while there are very good reasons for permitting it, in most cases it is the management that ushered the company into bankruptcy that is in charge of turning it around. Because trustees are not favored, there is really no regular procedure by which improvements in management personnel or techniques can be suggested or required. Generally, although the creditors moan and groan, everyone just stands back and waits for the Debtor to find financing, which it could not find before the bankruptcy; to become more proficient at what it does; and to improve its situation so dramatically that it quickly produces a bundle of extra money to pay its accumulated debts. Well, it happens!)

In any event, a major result of the Chapter 11 filing is that the company is required to disclose its most vital statistics and expose its methods of operations to the public, so that people like you can discover them for your own purposes.

In all federal districts, the Chapter 11 Debtor is required to make monthly reports respecting its business operations, which are filed with the Clerk of Court and the United States Trustee's office in the federal district in which the case was filed. Contrary to popular belief, the bankruptcy judge does not—and, by law, cannot—review the reports filed by the Debtor. The judge does not learn about the Debtor unless and until parties have a dispute that results in adversarial activity in court.

While the formats of the reports vary somewhat from district to district, they generally seek similar information about the Debtor's operations. (See Appendix C, the report required in the Northern District of Illinois [encompassing Chicago] entitled "Debtor in Possession [DIP] Operating Report—Summary of Cash Receipts and Disbursements; Statements of Aged Payables and Receivables." It provides a type of profit/loss statement for the month as well as cumulative figures for the operations during the bankruptcy case to date.)

The requirement that these reports be filed is designed to require the Debtor to disclose its basic operating information, so that creditors and the United States Trustee may monitor the Debtor for compliance with bankruptcy strictures. Those parties want to be sure that the Debtor has not:

(1) borrowed money without prior court approval;

(2) made payments to officers, directors, or owners outside the ordinary course of business;

(3) provided excessive compensation or expense reimbursement to any officer or employee;

(4) paid any pre-petition creditors, unless allowed by prior court order; or

(5) operated at a loss, so that "cost of administration" debts (payables arising during the bankruptcy case) build up to the detriment of the pre-petition creditors.

Upon request of the U.S. Trustee or any creditor, the bankruptcy judge may convert the case to a Chapter 7 liquidation for failure to file reports in a timely manner. Upon request, the judge may also convert the case to a Chapter 7 if the reports show continuing losses. A judge will sometimes appoint a Chapter 11 trustee if the reports show gross mismanagement or prove to be materially false.

The bankruptcy code recognizes that creditors may organize themselves to better protect their interests.

Primarily, the code provides for the formation of an Unsecured Creditors' Committee. The United States Trustee appoints the members of the committee by soliciting the interest of the larger unsecured creditors. With court approval, the committee may then retain counsel and, in larger cases, accountants and/or other professional consultants. The fees and costs of such professionals are to be borne by the Debtor. This can be a large burden in contentious cases. The members of the committee must bear their own expenses.

The committee is usually comprised of three to eleven members, depending on the size of the case. The ideal Unsecured Creditors' Committee, as conceptualized by the drafters of the bankruptcy code, is one that has on it representatives of the major unsecured creditor factions: creditors with small claims, as well as the major creditors; trade creditors and unsecured lenders; etc. As a practical matter, most creditors do not clamor to be on the committee, and the U.S. Trustee merely appoints anyone who is willing to serve.

Although permitted by the code, it is unusual to see court-approved committees in addition to the Unsecured Creditors' Committee. However, in very large cases the court may also recognize committees of debenture holders, special claimants (such as state governments or franchisees) and/or special classes of unsecured creditors (such as product liability plaintiffs, when those claims were a major cause of the bankruptcy).

The committees have a fiduciary duty to protect the interests of their constituents. They meet as necessary to consider reactions to the Debtor's actions, to plan for court hearings, to respond to the Debtor's proposed Plan of Reorganization, and to weigh possible aggressive actions against the Debtor in the bankruptcy court. Most of the implementation is accomplished through attorneys chosen by the committees.

While the Unsecured Creditors' Committee can be a thorn in the Debtor's side, more often than not it is actually helpful. The creditors on the committee, being the larger creditors, are not usually in a rush to see the value of their claims disappear through a liquidation. The committee provides a sounding board for reorganization proposals, and so gives the Debtor a pretty good idea as to what will be acceptable. Once a Plan of Reorganization is filed, if the committee approves, it will recommend to the unsecured creditors that they vote to accept the plan and thus virtually assure sufficient unsecured creditor votes to carry that class of creditor.

In spite of the potential for the Unsecured Creditors' Committee to be a key player, it is more the rule than the exception for such committees to be inept and ineffective. I have seen a committee fail to police requirements that the executive/owners cut their compensation during the bankruptcy case and then erroneously turn down the better offer in a bidding contest for a Chapter 11 company. In another case, I saw a committee refuse to do anything in the face of a Debtor's blatant fraud, even though it resulted in losing an outside purchaser who would have provided the unsecured creditors a substantial dividend.

In many cases with unsecured debt of less than $500,000, and some larger cases, the unsecured creditors do not show enough interest or organization to form an Unsecured Creditors' Committee. Although this results in a lack of feedback to the Debtor that may lead to an unpleasant surprise at plan voting time, on the plus side it often indicates that the creditors are demoralized and will not cause the Debtor much trouble.

While it is theoretically possible to reorganize in the face of contingent or unliquidated liabilities, as a practical matter the Debtor and the creditors usually need to know the exact debts to determine the best course of action for the company. As a result, the disputes that have been building up during the company's slide into bankruptcy must be brought to a head.

Many debts under dispute before the filing of the bankruptcy case are conceded by the Debtor. Of course, many were merely a smoke-screen set up by the Debtor because it couldn't pay its debts in a timely manner. Such disputes are not contested in the bankruptcy. Also, as the Debtor looks ahead to paying only a fraction of unsecured creditors' claims through a Plan of Reorganization, modest differences of opinion over the amount of any given debt become uneconomical to litigate. It is cheaper to concede.

However, larger disputes over larger debts must be resolved. Sometimes one major disputed claim is the cause of the bankruptcy. If litigation is already pending in another court, the bankruptcy judge has the discretion to allow that litigation to proceed there or to bring it into bankruptcy court—whichever will result in the most expeditious determination.

If no litigation is pending respecting a disputed claim, the Debtor either may object to the claim filed by the creditor or take the initiative and ask for determination of the claim by the bankruptcy judge. Such proceedings are handled in a "summary" manner so as not to delay the primary goal of the case, which is reorganization; pretrial procedures are expedited and the hearing may be less formal than a full trial. Thus, for better or for worse, disputes that may have taken years to litigate in a nonbankruptcy court—sometimes involving a good deal of money and sometimes requiring determination of complex legal issues and factual matters—may be disposed of quite quickly in a preemptory manner by the bankruptcy judge, so that the reorganization can proceed.

Of course, entering into battle with one's creditors may not be a wise course of action. After all, the Debtor will be needing their votes for a Plan of Reorganization. Consequently, the Debtor may trade its objection for a favorable vote by a creditor (which is probably illegal) or may not fight the claim at all. One common ploy is for the Debtor to provide in the Plan of Reorganization that claims can be objected to *after* confirmation of the plan, thus retaining a threat against creditors and saving the bloodshed until after the creditors have voted.

Then again, if a creditor with a large, disputed claim is highly unfriendly, the Debtor may have to succeed in reducing the amount of the claim or eliminating it altogether prior to the presentation of a Plan of Reorganization, to diminish the "no" vote.

The considerations of if, when, and how to litigate disputes are complicated by the existence of the bankruptcy case. The debtor-creditor dance becomes more complicated, but therefore more flexible and thus more favorable to the Debtor. That's what makes Chapter 11 practice so interesting!

The Plan of Reorganization is so central to a Chapter 11 case and to the purchase of, or investment in, a Chapter 11 company, that Chapter 11 (of course!) of this book is devoted entirely to it. However, I am including a few broad brushstrokes in this chapter to provide you with an overview.

The goal of a Chapter 11 case is the proposal and approval of a Plan of Reorganization that provides a program for dealing with the debts of the Debtor. Generally speaking, the debts of the company are held in abeyance until payment is made pursuant to such a plan.

The Debtor may file a plan at any time after the petition commencing the case is filed. After the expiration of an initial period during which only the Debtor may file a plan, the creditors are free to propose a plan and seek its approval. When plans are proposed by opposing factions, each one may be sent simultaneously to creditors for approval. Every plan circulated to creditors must be accompanied by a disclosure statement, in a form previously approved by the judge, that provides financial and other information about the Debtor's past, present, and hoped-for future.

The bankruptcy laws do not specify how much must be offered to creditors in a plan. However, there is a hierarchy of types of creditors, discussed more fully in Chapter 7, that generally dictates the relative bargaining strength of, and thus percentage payment to, each class of creditors.

Plan effectuation requires approval by creditors, in a manner more fully described in Chapter 11 of this book, and confirmation by the bankruptcy judge that the plan does not violate certain prohibitions in the bankruptcy code.

Chapter 5

Prospecting: How to Uncover the Values

Many people who understand that great values lie in the bankruptcy courts are nevertheless reluctant to go after them because they feel that, as "outsiders," they will not be able to penetrate the Bankruptcy Cabal. There is a widespread feeling that only a small circle of insiders control the system.

Speaking as a long-time bankruptcy lawyer, things are just not that well organized at the bankruptcy courts. While in each district there tends to be an easily definable group of lawyers who specialize in bankruptcy practice, respect and attention is given to anyone who shows an understanding of the rules of the game. The lawyers are always interested in dealing with a principal who may "make something happen" in a case, especially if he will fund a reorganization that, incidentally, covers their legal fees.

Also, outsiders vastly overestimate the community of interest among the bankruptcy lawyers. While specialists may get to know each other by toiling in the same fields, that does not mean that they all like each other. Also, while some of the old timers can be "back scratchers," most bankruptcy lawyers do just what they are supposed to do—represent their clients in the best way they know and let the chips fall where they may. (In any event, do retain a bankruptcy attorney to represent you at *least* at the later stages when you are about to make a firm offer for a target company.)

It may also seem daunting to be required to appear before a bankruptcy judge several times during the course of an acquisition of a company. However, keep in mind that *you are the hero!* You are the one who will be saving the company, making payments to creditors, and allowing the judge to close the case. The judge will understand your special place in the process and will do his best not to scare you away. Responsible, serious, prospective purchasers do not get treated shabbily by bankruptcy judges.

One reason that the system is not unfriendly to potential "angels" is that the judges and lawyers do not see a lot of them. There simply are no regular institutional buyers of Chapter 11 companies prowling the courts. Rather than a bother, the prospective purchaser is like a breath of fresh air blowing into the courtroom. While this book may increase the numbers of purchasers of Chapter 11 companies, the plain fact is that at this time the system is crying out for such people and few exist.

One other fact should not be overlooked: read this book, learn your lessons well, and jump into the fray, and soon you will be an "insider" yourself!

Once you have acquired a feel for the bankruptcy process and have located a possible Chapter 11 target, you will need to begin collecting information. The courthouse is a good place to start.

In general, papers filed with a court are subject to inspection by the public, and no one has to explain to court personnel why he or she wishes to review them. Whether the papers were presented to the clerk's office, the judge's clerk, or the judge, they are stamped as "received" or "filed" and placed in a court file.

Because of bankruptcy requirements, much information about Chapter 11 Debtors is "on the record," even for privately held companies. Consequently, it is possible to learn much about a Chapter 11 company before any overtures are made to management, simply by visiting the bankruptcy clerk's office at the federal courthouse in the district where the case was filed.

The specific procedures vary from district to district. In some districts, the judge maintains the court file in his chambers; in others, all papers end up in the clerk's office and the judge works with copies; and in yet others, the judge calls for all or part of a file as needed. Some inquiry may be required to learn the local customs, but soon you will be an expert.

A bankruptcy court file will contain a wide range of useful papers. For example, it will contain all informational documents that the Debtor is required to file, such as the Schedules and operating reports. It will also hold all notices; all motions, complaints, and responses; all legal briefs; and all evidence submitted to the court in contested matters. The court records also include all claims filed in the case, either in the general case file or in a separate claims file. Also, in order to avoid allegations of impropriety, most judges will place in the court file letters that they receive concerning the case and copies of any letters they (rarely) might write in response.

Unfortunately, court files are often incomplete, for one reason or another. The judge or the judge's law clerks may be using portions in connection with a hearing or writing a legal opinion. Papers may be in transit between clerks. Thoughtless people walk off with pleadings rather than taking the trouble to photocopy them. And, as with any other bureaucracy, things disappear into "black holes" in totally unexplainable ways.

In most districts, two alternative sources act as supplements and checklists for the court file: the "case docket" and the "claims docket." As soon as a document is received by a court clerk's office, it is logged onto a list—a "docket"—as a record of its existence separate from the file. The claims docket will disclose the date each claim was filed, the name and address of the creditor, and the amount and type of the claim. The other papers filed in a case will be listed in the case docket in chronological order and identified either by title (e.g., "Debtor's Motion to Employ Accountants") or short summary (e.g., "Order authorizing sale of certain assets"). A quick trip to the photocopying machine, and you have two handy reference lists. During the next several years the clerks' offices will be moving to computerized dockets.

If you are following the fortunes of a Chapter 11 company for any period of time, do not forget to update your docket lists. The bankruptcy court clerk in many districts will accept telephone inquiries if they are reasonably limited in scope. For example, in Chicago there are ten case docket clerks, one for each last digit (0-9) in the case numbers, each with his or her own direct-dial telephone number. The clerk will provide docket information to the caller.

The "Schedules of Assets and Liabilities" in the court file provide a detailed balance sheet of the Chapter 11 company's condition *as of the date of the filing of the bankruptcy case.* From that form you can determine, for example, whether the company owns its place of business or other real estate and the amounts of any mortgages; the nature and amount of priority tax claims; the identity of secured and unsecured creditors; the existence of any patents held by the company; and the value, but not an itemized list, of equipment, machinery, inventory, and accounts receivable. A required attachment to the schedules lists the Debtor's ongoing contractual obligations, such as leases of equipment and premises. (See Chapters 6 and 7 for a more detailed analysis of assets and liabilities of Chapter 11 companies.)

Operating reports of the Chapter 11 Debtor, which amount to profit/ loss statements, are also placed in the court file. Although the most recent report in a file is usually a month or so out of date, the operating reports nevertheless provide insight into the level of the company's receipts and the nature of its overhead. They also list the gross amount of receivable and payables. If the Debtor has been in Chapter 11 for any length of time, a chronological review of the reports quickly discloses whether a company's situation is improving, deteriorating, or stabilizing, and whether it is operating on a profitable, unprofitable, or break-even basis.

Other court papers in the file can provide fascinating insight into the Debtor's problems. The landlord may complain that rentals are not being paid and ask that the Debtor be evicted. Perhaps a secured creditor has filed a complaint asking that the court lift the "automatic stay" (the injunction against creditor collection activities that is imposed automatically and without the need for a court order immediately upon a debtor's filing of bankruptcy) and allow that creditor to foreclose on its collateral. Perhaps the Unsecured Creditors' Committee has requested the appointment of a trustee. The Debtor may have objected to the claim of a large creditor. Memoranda supporting motions may contain tales of woe. Remember, however, that while such pleadings can provide you with "red flags" marking issues that should be explored, they are adversarial statements of parties' legal positions and should not necessarily be accepted as truth unless and until the judge makes findings and issues determinative orders.

One way of estimating the reliability of the Debtor's Schedules is to compare the Debtor's listing of debts in the Schedules with claims actually filed by creditors and located in the court file. Most of the claims will be on forms entitled "Proof of Claim," the content of which is prescribed by the bankruptcy code (see Appendix D). However, claims in any recognizable form are generally accepted as valid. While the accuracy of creditors' filed claims may be as dubious as the Debtor's listing of debts—creditors are prone to inflate claims to counter the discounted payment they are likely to receive through the bankruptcy—a legitimate claim will have attached invoices or other reasonably reliable evidence of the existence and amount of the debt.

After allowing for some inflation, wide variation between claims as filed and debts as listed is a "red flag" marking unreliability of the Debtor's financial information, serious disputes over claims, or both.

Note that the period to file claims in a Chapter 11 is open ended. A cutoff date—known in bankruptcy parlance as a "bar date" —is set only by order of the bankruptcy judge, either as part of consideration of a proposed Plan of Reorganization or upon request of a party (usually the Debtor). Thus you can never be sure of the total claims in a case until the bar date has passed and all disputes over claims have been determined by the court. You continually should be updating your claims docket list and reviewing claims in the file.

A comparison between the docket lists and the court file should tell you if anything is missing. If the missing documents are important to your review, check with the clerks who might be using them for one reason or other. If all you have acquired by the end of your search is a collection of shrugs from the court personnel, you can try the U.S. Trustee's office, which has copies of many, but not all, court papers. If that fails, you will have to contact one of the attorneys of record in the case.

Speaking of attorneys, when reviewing the court records you should make a list of the attorneys of record and whom they represent. You will find the list useful in keeping the players straight and when contacting individuals for further information. Most attorneys central to the case will file an "appearance" on a designated court form, which states the attorney's name, address, and telephone number and the name of the client whom the attorney represents. Court rules also require each pleading filed to contain that same information about the party's attorney.

Do not be too discouraged after your initial investigation. Remember that companies go into Chapter 11 because they have troubles that they have not been able to solve, and often their history is chaotic and their debts are out of line with their assets. Remember that you may be the key to bringing order to the company's operations, and the debt picture will be greatly changed upon the company's emergence from Chapter 11. Concentrate upon the "gold" hidden in the dross and how you may extricate it for your benefit.

Of course, the court records can only provide you with the bare facts of a Debtor's past and present. If your "business nose" tells you that the company may provide a good opportunity, the next step is to speak with some of the players.

If you cannot determine from a review of the file and docket sheets what the outcome of a hearing was or whether a certain order was entered, etc., the judge's secretary, docket clerk, or law clerk may know the answer. Sometimes you can get the judge's law clerk or the assistant U.S. Trustee to give you their views of the Debtor's situation, or other editorial comments, while responding to your requests for factual information.

As to which of the main players to contact first, try the president of the Chapter 11 company unless you know some other officer or director. While it might be tempting to go to the Unsecured Creditor's Committee or the Debtor's primary lender, such tactics will immediately poison any possible relationship with the Debtor, and you should hold those types of actions in reserve. Besides, if you ignore the Debtor in your initial contacts, you might be making it hard on yourself—the principals of the Chapter 11 Debtor may be more than happy to take in an investor or sell the company and may welcome your overture with open arms.

While it is recommended you contact the Debtor first, do not necessarily lay all your cards on the table. A vague response by you that you heard about the company "through the grapevine" may go over better than confessing that you are scouring the courthouse for good bankruptcy deals. More importantly, leave the issue of whether you are an "investor" or "purchaser" ambiguous.

The whitest hat to wear is that of the investor—that is, as someone who may provide capital and become a partner or shareholder along with the present owner—rather than as someone who is going to steal the owner's "baby." It will be easier to gain information about the target company from the owner. Also, while you may think that you want nothing to do with management that has already shown failure, you may find that the chemistry is right and that the present owner has important skills to offer going forward even though it may be you who provides the impetus for turning around the company. For another alternative, in a small percentage of cases you may learn that the only problem was lack of capital, and you may be content becoming a relatively passive investor.

You can make your questioning of management as direct or subtle as fits your style, but there is no point in being too shy or too Mr. Nice Guy. Your job is to get to the bottom of the company's problems and to discover its strong points, and so, let the questions fly. Otherwise, you are wasting your time.

Even where your inquiry has been well received by the Debtor, at some point after you have established a relationship and you have confirmed your preliminary interest in the company, you will wish to initiate contact with the major creditors. While the Debtor's management will be none too pleased—and may try a number of arguments to keep you isolated from the creditors—you must make it clear that it is time for you to find out what those creditors will require from a Plan of Reorganization. You should not place sole reliance upon the Debtor's assessment for too long, or you might be in for a nasty surprise when you propose your purchase price. Remember, the truth is most likely a composite of the parties' views and positions.

Of course, your overture to the company owner may be rebuffed in no uncertain terms. You may be told that the owner is doing just fine, thank you, and that he will be turning the company around himself. That attitude is more likely to prevail when the Chapter 11 petition has been filed only recently. (Of course, the owner may be right—but only in the minority of cases.) You may be able to persuade the owner to talk to you by dangling the possibility of financial help, but, if not, you should not attempt to force yourself on him.

If you have received no encouragement from the owner, you may choose to bide your time, monitoring the court file and waiting until the early-case optimism has faded. The owner who tells you to get lost in the first telephone call may have a more reasonable response to your third.

For example, about six months ago while rooting around the courthouse, I came upon a Chapter 11 case of a company that manufactures glass products. When I contacted the Debtor's bankruptcy attorney I was informed that, while the owners had been convinced that they must sell the company due to their inability to make it profitable, the company had recently had a few good months in sales and so there were renewed hopes of an internally generated turnaround. I filed the case away in the back of my brain, and on occasions when I crossed paths with the attorney, I always inquired as to the financial health of his client. Recently he advised me that those good months had been followed by a few bad months and now, reality having reared its ugly head, the owners were once more willing—anxious—to find a suitor. One of my clients is now investigating the company for possible acquisition.

If you are at the stage when you want to make something happen, you may then make inquiries to the major secured lender, the

Unsecured Creditors' Committee, and/or the major unsecured creditors. In fact, the ability to negotiate with persons who are not the owners or executives of the target company is one important advantage of pursuing a company that is in Chapter 11. If one or more of those parties sponsor your investigation and bid, through bankruptcy procedures you may be able to buy the company over the owner's objections!

The major secured lender—usually a bank—is almost always a key to the takeover of a company in bankruptcy, because of the exalted status of lien creditors. (See more detailed discussion of the hierarchy of claims in Chapter 7.) Since secured claims ordinarily must be paid substantially in full, you must verify the amount of the bank's claim. Also, you should lay the groundwork for persuading the bank to grant you a continuation of the loan, and/or a fresh loan, rather than cashing in its chips.

Since most Chapter 11 petitions are filed after a long period of creditor strife and attendant damage to the Debtor's goodwill, most likely you will find the banker quite anxious (undoubtedly in his own low-key way) to dump the present owner and executives. Do not forget that, by indicating to the target company's banker that you may be interested in purchasing or investing in the business, you are suddenly presenting him with an option which will help him clean up his sullied loan portfolio. Nor does it escape his notice that you have the potential to become a good customer.

The observations of a frustrated banking officer can prove most useful. By starting off asking questions with answers "on the record" (such as details of the bank's claim) and moving to inquiries requiring more subjective answers (such as whether the banker thinks that the Debtor as presently constituted can successfully reorganize), you no doubt will gain significant insight into the target company. Be sure to ask the banker why he thinks the business ran into trouble.

For some reason which might not be immediately obvious, the banker might give you a cool reception and so it may take some time to establish a relationship. You may want to ask for a meeting to discuss whether the bank's interests and yours coincide. Certainly, any legitimate name-dropping you can do, such as providing banking references, will increase the banker's comfort level and start him thinking that maybe he has a "live one" to be cultivated and encouraged.

With the Unsecured Creditors' Committee, you do not have to be too subtle about your desire to take over the Debtor. The committee is usually short on information but long on desire to (a) talk to someone who will pay them something on their claims, (b) throw out the bums now running the Debtor, or (c) both of the above. However, be warned that it is not unusual for the Debtor to have a "mole" on the committee, and your existence and attitude may be reported to the executives of the target company.

The committee usually is not helpful to you in pinning down the total of unsecured claims, but you may be able to find out what dividend the unsecured creditors are hoping for. The savvier the members of the committee, the sooner they will acknowledge the paltry percentage that they can expect, even in a takeover situation.

Your initial contact with the Unsecured Creditors' Committee should be with the chairman, whose name, address, and telephone number is usually disclosed in the official notice of the appointment of the committee which is placed in the court file by the U.S. Trustee's office. If you cannot locate the notice, a telephone call to the U.S. Trustee's office in the court district where the case was filed will produce the information. The chairman may ask you to meet with him or attend the next committee meeting, and, as with your approach to the banker, it will never hurt to shamelessly flaunt your credentials as someone with the wherewithal to rehabilitate the Debtor. (Do not forget that most creditors are suppliers of goods or services to the Debtor and look forward to making profits through future sales to the reorganized company.)

In the event that no Unsecured Creditors' Committee has been apppointed, you can contact the larger unsecured creditors individually. The court papers will show which unsecured creditors are taking an active part in the case (usually through attorneys). Also, a review of the schedules will disclose the larger unsecured creditors who might be expected to take an interest in you and who may take the lead in promoting your cause. If the schedules have not yet been filed, you might review a form that the Debtor is required to file at the onset of the case, the "List of Twenty Largest Unsecured Creditors," which the U.S. Trustee uses when inviting creditors to form the Unsecured Creditors' Committee in the case.

In dealing with the unsecured creditors, you have multiple goals. On the one hand, you want to take advantage of your incipient status as a potential savior of the company and funder of creditor dividends, in order to acquire information from the creditors and build a constituency. On the other hand, ever so subtly you should prepare them to take a big "hit," so that when you propose your purchase price, they will be prepared and will not foolishly refuse to negotiate at your price level.

In addition to providing you with viewpoints, the creditors are in a position to actively help your investigation. By law, any creditor may request to review the Debtor's books, records, other documents, and so the committee or any major creditor can usually obtain copies of basic financial documents, such as balance sheets, for the asking. Such a creditor can pose questions to management on your behalf. A creditor might even demand a tour of the plant and a review of the Chapter 11 company's books and records and bring you along.

Aside from "fronting" for you, creditors may legitimately promote your interests. It is not particularly unusual to find an Unsecured Creditors' Committee that reserves its rights to respond to inquiries of potential purchasers, and even to *generate* the interest of potential purchasers. The answer to the owner's howl of protest is twofold: first, it was the owner who put the company into play by filing a Chapter 11; and (usually), since the balance sheet of the Debtor shows a negative shareholders' equity, it is the creditors, and not the shareholders, who have the biggest stake in the company. Sometimes, there is a third response to the owner: you are a loser, and we would not mind losing you.

Another variation on the theme is the "most-favored-friends" ploy. You may have an initially favorable relationship with the Debtor's owner, only to find out that his view is that "my million hours of work is worth a million dollars," or some other concept that places the purchase price at an unrealistically high level. If no one can persuade him to voluntarily lower the price, you may decide that your best friend in the case is not the owner but the Unsecured Creditors' Committee. If the committee gets too pushy, you might decide that your only friend is the bank. (Remember, once the "exclusive period" is over, any creditor may sponsor a Plan of Reorganization.) The situation may be ripe to play off the parties' interests, conflicts, and fears against each other. Of course, you may wreak havoc in the case, but you just might end up with a purchase at a very satisfying price!

So far the discussion in this section has centered upon communications with the *parties,* as contrasted with their *attorneys.* Generally, businessperson-to-businessperson contacts are more productive, especially since most of the attorneys' knowledge about the Debtor is derivative. However, you may have questions about the status of specific motions or other courtroom activities, and there is no rule that says that you cannot contact a party's attorney. If you are represented by an attorney who is part of the local clique of bankruptcy specialists, an attorney-to-attorney relationship may expedite matters. However, as a lawyer I can appreciate the benefits of getting the lawyers for the other parties involved only after a certain amount of progress has been made.

Certainly your own attorneys and accountants can be a big help to you at all stages. Remember, your obligations upon purchasing a business will be quite sizeable, and those professionals can steer you clear of pitfalls and advise you of "tricks of the trade." In particular, your bankruptcy attorney can help you develop tactics and strategies and point the way through the bankruptcy court procedures.

Ultimately, how much you use those professionals, and when, will depend on your own methods and tastes. However, it is best not to legally commit yourself to purchase or invest in a Chapter 11 company without first, at some stage, having an accountant review the financial information and a *bankruptcy* lawyer advise you of the legalities. Do not be penny-wise and dollar foolish. In other words, if used properly, professionals do not cost money, they save money. In still other words, the use of professionals is "cheap insurance."

Chapter 6

Investigating the Assets

When investigating the assets of a target company, you should never forget what the magician does with seemingly solid, material objects—he makes them disappear or changes them into something else before your very eyes. Some business people can create similar illusions.

There will be no detailed discussion here of the techniques for reading business-related financial records. There are books on the market solely devoted to analyzing financial information, some related to the buying or selling of a business. Go out and buy at least one as a companion to this book.

This is not to underestimate in any way the value of reviewing financial records of all types. Very often an owner will make inaccurate oral statements or gross generalizations in negotiations that are not supported by documentation. Also, it is very useful to make a chronological collection of a company's financial records and to note the changes.

The primary financial statements are the "Balance Sheet" (listing assets and liabilities as of a specific date) and the "Profit/Loss Statement" (listing income and expenses for a given period). They should be in a customary format that follows recognized bookkeeping rules. It is common for companies to prepare such statements quarterly, and many companies even do it monthly. At a very minimum, a company should have a balance sheet and profit/loss statement prepared as of the end of each fiscal year. If a company cannot produce formal, businesslike statements with reasonable frequency, that is a "red flag" that the owners do not truly know their financial situation and nothing that they say about their assets, liabilities, or operations can be trusted.

When reviewing financial statements, always remember the huge difference in reliability between audited and unaudited statements.

While unaudited statements are supposed to be based totally on competent underlying records, basically, the company is "on its honor" to be accurate. If an accountant prepares an unaudited financial statement, he is merely taking the information *provided to him by the company* and arranging it in a professional format. He does not verify its truthfulness. While you may choose to accept that information at face value in your early investigations, if you are serious about purchasing or investing in a company, you or your accountant should investigate carefully to be sure that the information on the financial statements conforms with the company's underlying documents, and that the system of generating those underlying records contains safeguards and is likely to produce accurate figures.

On the other hand, a statement produced as a result of an audit by accountants is considered to be very reliable. In fact, the accounting firm certifies the accuracy of the information in an audited statement. That is because the accountants come onto the company's premises, review the underlying operating documents, sample the inventory, and run cross-checks on the different types of financial records. The accountants do not accept management's word but rather verify the information to their satisfaction. Thus, while there have been spectacular exceptions when accountants have been bribed or have otherwise taken part in a fraud, generally speaking an audited statement is considered the final word. The reputation of the accounting firm stands as your assurance of accuracy; however, its professional liability insurance policy provides the ultimate degree of comfort!

Potential purchasers or investors frequently request that a company without audited statements undergo an audit to certify the accuracy of the company's figures. However, audits are relatively expensive—especially the initial one—and almost invariably the request is refused.

One recent case in which I represented prospective purchasers of a manufacturing company drove home the differences between audited and unaudited statements quite strongly. Supposedly in order to save accounting fees and because the owner of the company was a certified public accountant, the company had ceased receiving yearly audits several years prior to the filing of its Chapter 11 case. However, when one of the prospective purchasers, himself an accountant, reviewed the balance sheets and profit/loss statements, he realized that huge descrepancies were carefully hidden and hundreds of thousands of dollars of assets had simply disappeared off the books. No one knows how to "cook" the books like an accountant-turned-owner! Not only did I renew my wariness of unaudited statements, I gained a greater appreciation of the help that an accountant can provide to prospective purchasers of companies.

Although not in customary form, the Schedules of Assets and Liabilities that a company is required to file in a Chapter 11 proceeding amounts to a balance sheet as of the date of the filing of the petition. Because of the categories mandated by the official bankruptcy form (see Appendix A), the schedules may actually provide greater insight than a standard balance sheet.

While the schedules can provide balance sheet information, because of their very nature treat that information at a level of reliability slightly *below* that of an unaudited financial statement. Because many standard bookkeeping formats do not match the listings in the schedules, at times a company's records are not in a form that allows accurate culling of information. Also, unfortunately, many bankruptcy lawyers—and, thus, their clients—do not view schedules as something to be held to balance-sheet accounting standards. Accordingly, the schedules are often slapped together with no real commitment to accuracy or full disclosure.

Another note of caution: even assuming good faith, the schedules consist of the *Debtor's view* of its liabilities and *estimate* of the fair market value of its assets. The quality of the information can vary widely. It should not be forgotten that a root cause of bankruptcy for many small companies is the lack of good financial record keeping. While of course it is a federal crime to hide assets, inaccurate valuations in the schedules do not ordinarily provoke sanctions as long as there is some minimal basis for the "guesstimation."

Consequently, while the schedules provide a good starting point, they should not be read with an unquestioning eye. You will quickly learn to recognize the schedules that are based on solid bookkeeping and those that are vague guesstimates.

In conclusion, while financial records provide useful insight into a company, do not take them as The Gospel. Look for inconsistencies and the care with which they are produced. Determine early whether you can rely on them for providing an accurate picture, or whether you must dig deeper and use other resources to understand the company's financial situation.

First let us deal with the "subjective realities" involving a company's assets. While you may receive a tour of the plant early on, mostly you will be dealing with various forms of written information in which the assets are quantified by dollar amount or listed descriptively. You are assuming the reality behind the abstract symbols contained on the sheets of paper.

Leaving aside the question of outright fraud, for which you always should be vigilant, the valuation of physical—or "hard"—assets on the balance sheet seldom is the final word. Generally accepted accounting procedures require that physical assets be listed by purchase price, from which depreciation is then subtracted, leaving a net "book value." While those requirements allow for orderly and easily calculable statistics, they do not necessarily give you a bearing on the "real" value of the assets.

The practical businessperson will treat the "fair market value" of an asset as the real value. Fair market value is defined as the price that a willing buyer will pay, and a willing seller will accept, in a situation where neither party is forced by circumstances to act. In other words, if you own a piece of machinery, what offer would entice you to part with it? You would take into account the price and the ease of acquiring a like (used) piece of equipment, and possibly the incremental additional cost of acquiring an unused piece. If the piece is working beautifully in your assembly line and a replacement would be hard to find, that machine might be very valuable *to you*.

Outside forces may affect the fair market value of assets greatly. During the Carter presidency, rampant inflation caused new equipment prices to rise so dramatically that used machinery prices rose also, to the point where the market price of used machinery often exceeded its purchase price several years earlier. During the Reagan years, accelerated depreciation allowances—really a corporate tax break—resulted in very low book values that had the effect of exaggerating the diminution in the value of equipment and machinery caused by actual physical use and obsolescence. Equipment or machinery required for the particular industry that you are investigating may be custom made or manufactured by only one or two companies, creating a high replacement cost and thus driving up the value of the pieces already on the shop floor. Conversely, new processes or foreign competition may have the effect of placing a factory at a competitive disadvantage, driving down its market price. Hard assets simply do not have hard values.

In fact, the winds of change can render hard assets valueless, to the point where they become liabilities because it costs money to get rid of them. One example of such an asset-valuation roller coaster ride is instructive.

Oil was scarce in the United States in the late 1970s due to OPEC actions, and refineries only grudgingly sold diesel tractor fuel to farmers. A number of large agricultural cooperatives, figuring that they could not lose, pooled their resources and purchased an oil refinery in the Midwest. For several years the refinery, valued at approximately $500 million, was successful, but then in the early 1980s disunity in OPEC caused oil prices to slip. Suddenly, other refineries were after the farmer market. Slight differences in efficiencies and capabilities of refineries became all-important. The result: the farmers bought their fuel elsewhere, the cooperative-owned refinery lost its market and could not find any others, and a $500 million refinery became a useless heap of metal. It was demolished recently by its bankruptcy trustee, at substantial cost to the creditors and/or the owners. (They are still fighting about it.)

The Moral of the Story: while book value provides general information about the purchase price and years of use of machinery and equipment, valuation for purposes of the purchase of a business requires a more sophisticated analysis, which takes into account the usefulness to the company and extraneous conditions.

Chapter 11 complicates the valuation of hard assets, although usually to the prospective purchaser's advantage. The practical value of the hard assets in the hands of the unprofitable company becomes diminished. Because of the uncertainty respecting the Debtor's future which is brought into focus by the filing of the bankruptcy, what were formerly viewed as solid operating assets by the creditors suddenly begin to look like scrap metal. Consequently, in negotiations the prospective buyer may publicly value the hard assets at a level only modestly above liquidation (auction sale) value, while at the same time privately valuing them much higher based upon their usefulness to the reorganized business under new management. The wider the disparity, the better the deal.

You may have noted that nothing has been said about appraisals. Appraisers, whether they specialize in real estate and have formal credentials or whether they are dealers in machinery and equipment, are simply experts who bring their knowledge of contemporary, comparable sales to the table. As with any knowledgeable consultant, their advice can be valuable—but there are two problems.

The first problem with appraisers is the expense. It is not cheap to have a good appraiser do (and this is the key) a *thorough* job. Ideally, the appraiser should review a number of sales of the same or very similar items, in similar condition, in nondistressed situations as well as auctions. Locating a sufficient number of comparable sales is not very easy. Much attention must be paid to establishing similarities and to calculating the economic effects of dissimilarities. As a practical matter, most business buyers are not inclined to pay the cost of an appraisal of business machinery and equipment, although real estate appraisals are used a little more frequently.

The second problem is that, alas, the process is not an exact science. In extreme situations, such as court contests over the value of a business or piece of real estate, it is not uncommon for the opposing appraisers to have widely divergent opinions, each (surprise!) closely matching the previously filed pleadings of his sponsor. In uncontested situations, perhaps the appraisers' opinions are more objective, but I have seen too many conflicting appraisals in court to be comfortable relying heavily upon the judgment of an appraiser.

Of course, much lower on the scale of reliablity is management's view of the condition of the machinery and equipment. To hear them tell it, the operating assets all work in perfect harmony, were purchased yesterday and maintained by an army of mechanics, and never, ever, break down. In the process of telling, the collecting of chugging antiques is transformed into an assembly line for which the Japanese would lust.

Do not be fooled by the illusionists. As Marvin Gaye cautioned in "I Heard It Through the Grapevine," believe half of what you see and none of what you hear. It is well worth a prospective purchaser's time to spend a number of days on the premises viewing the operations.

While inventory has a physical, countable existence, inherently its valuation is more problematical than that of machinery and equipment; and valuation in the context of a troubled company presents problems that are even more acute than in the ordinary business situation.

The first problem deals with its actual existence. Companies vary widely in the frequency with which they take physical counts of inventory. Well-run companies go long periods between taking inventory but have sophisticated methods of attributing inventories statistically. Poorly run companies, such as those that find themselves in Chapter 11, do not want to "waste" money taking actual counts of assets and have only general impressions of items in stock. The prospective purchaser or investor should question management closely to determine the likely relationship between the figures on the inventory lists and reality. It is prudent to run at least a few sample counts.

Be sure to evaluate the obsolescence of the inventory. Raw inventory is only as valuable as its usefulness in creating a saleable product. Many companies, particularly unsuccessful ones, carry substantial amounts of useless raw inventory on the books; they do not get rid of it and write it off because then the banker will get excited and demand additional collateral, or worse. The company may list work-in-progress separately, but in a distressed company the "work" often stays "in progress" a long time. If the inventory is related to unsuccessful product lines, how much of it will be useful with the products you intend to produce?

A major reason to exercise prudence when investigating the hard assets is that, as a practical matter, the chances for enforcing any warranties or representations made by the Chapter 11 seller are remote. The judge may find valuation too subjective a matter to award damages. Further, assuming purchase of the whole business, nothing will remain against which to make a claim. Also, while under the law the owner and executives of the selling company are personally liable for their fraud, in many cases because of the prior financial problems of the company, they are tapped out. Consequently, more reliance should be placed on actual investigation and less placed on representations and warranties than in an ordinary purchase.

A number of assets on the balance sheet have no physical form at all— they exist only on paper.

Accounts receivable, being sums due from customers for completed sales, would seem to be an asset whose "real" value equals its book value, but unfortunately life is not so simple. Accounts that take longer than thirty days to collect should be discounted to reflect the cost of money, and at some point—usually 180 days—accounts are deemed to be uncollectible and thus worthless. An "aging" schedule, one which divides accounts receivable by whether they are thirty, sixty, ninety, etc., days old, highlights the company's ability to turn its receivables into receipts.

Accounts receivable of a Chapter 11 company must be given closer scrutiny than those of successful business because often aged receivables are a symptom of one or more of the company's problems. The easiest problem to solve is that caused by inattention to collection procedures, because better practices can be instituted. Many times management is blind to the fact that the differences between profitability and Chapter 11 is the percentage by which collections lag behind the industry average.

The more difficult situation is when the receivables problem is really the symptom of another, more fundamental problem. Companies sometimes intentionally or unintentionally establish a pattern of selling to poor credit risks without sufficient concern for payment. Thus it is not so much the collectibility of receivables that is a problem as it is the legitimacy of the sales themselves. Another possibility is that the receivables problem is really a production problem, if customers are *refusing* to pay for goods that they claim are deficient in some manner.

A sophisticated approach is to go beyond the paperwork and to telephone overdue account debtors (with the Chapter 11 company's approval) under the guise of asking for payment. A sampling should tell you whether payments are not being made because of account debtors' problems (a bad enough situation) or because of disputes between the Chapter 11 vendor and the product purchasers (a "red flag" situation).

So much can be learned by talking with customers of the target company that the company's executives may vehemently object. That form of innvestigation may have to wait until you can demand to do it as final verification before making a firm offer. The owners may require you to make an offer first and then to verify accounts receivable as a "contingency" for closing.

Accounting entries for such abstract assets as "patents and copyrights," "trademarks," and "goodwill" are permitted by generally accepted accounting procedures. They exist as evidence that the business has made expenditures to develop products whose uniqueness is protected by law (patents and copyrights) or to develop its image with its customers (trademarks and goodwill). Most companies carry these assets at their cost, i.e., the amount of money that the company has spent in developing them. Unfortunately, their cost usually has nothing whatsoever to do with their actual value to that business and so, once again, you must do your own analysis of the "real" value of such bookkeeping entries.

As may be expected, the usefulness of such items easily can be nil. Huge sums may be spent on a patented doohickey only to find out that the world is not beating a path to the patentholder's door. A trademarked logo may come to be identified by the customer with a poorly run Chapter 11 company. Goodwill has to be the softest of the "soft" assets.

But take heart. There are some positive elements in what thus far has been "watch out, it is probably worth less than its book value." Soft assets such as patents, copyrights, trademarks, and goodwill may have hidden value that only you may recognize is not fool's gold.

While it is unlikely that the true value of a patent or a copyright is equal to its development cost, it may very well be that its value is far *greater* to you. Of course, its value to the troubled company has been diminished because such a business usually lacks the funds to continue its development and support it with an adequate marketing program; and because it is tied to a Chapter 11 Debtor, the creditors may have written it down in their calculations to something close to zero. However, you may realize that it can be quite valuable if developed and supported properly or if sold to a major corporation. In other words, once you have liberated it from its attachment to a troubled company, its full value can be realized.

Hidden value in trademarks and goodwill are more problematical, but can exist in a limited circumstance, namely when the company is a household (or industry-wide) name and it has not squandered its goodwill during its slide downhill. There are numerous examples of companies that have been purchased virtually solely for their name recognition. While such businesses are ordinarily in need of a great deal of restructuring, they can provide a vehicle for your entry into a particular market.

Continuing obligations required of the Debtor actually may be beneficial. If real estate or equipment lease rental payments are below market rates, through the Plan of Reorganization the company may choose to remain as a lessee even over the lessor's objection. If lease obligations are onerous, the lease may be "rejected" through a Chapter 11 Plan of Reorganization. Thus the reorganized company should have the benefit of a satisfactory lease situation, whichever way is most advantageous. The same may be done with other contracts, such as equipment installment purchases.

Another positive negative is the "net operating loss," commonly referred to as the "n.o.l." The n.o.l. appears at the bottom of the year-end profit/loss statement in the event that a company has failed to make a profit. Companies in Chapter 11 commonly have several successive years of n.o.l.'s. The positive aspect of an n.o.l. is that, with certain limitations, the Internal Revenue Code allows unprofitable corporations to "bank" their n.o.l.'s and apply them against future profits.

Thus a company with substantial prior losses may enjoy several years of "sheltered" nontaxable profits.

There is only one trouble with n.o.l.'s—Uncle Sam does not like people to deal in them. It is not possible for a new controlling owner to have the advantage of an n.o.l. that was created by the prior owner. Therefore, upon a change of controlling ownership (greater than fifty percent), the corporate entity loses the benefit of the n.o.l. The same is true if the company totally changes its line of business. (This is a simplified summary. The rules actually are quite technical.)

It's not fair, you say, for the corporate entity to be punished for an ownership change. Such a policy, you say, violates the legal concept of the corporation as an entity legally separate from its owners. Tough, says the I.R.S.; thou shalt not buy a company for its n.o.l.

That the n.o.l. is sitting out there on the corporate tree like a financial plum, ripe for the picking, usually drives the prospective purchasers crazy. Much time and energy—and money for accountants' fees—are spent considering stratagems for taking over a company and retaining the n.o.l.. However, I have never seen a legitimate method of accomplishing both goals that the accountants will guarantee to pass muster with the I.R.S. What usually happens is that the purchaser must discount the n.o.l. to near zero, and then if the stratagem succeeds— which the purchaser will not know for several years—the n.o.l. will become the "gravy" on the deal.

There is a good deal of temptation to phony up the deal by retaining the prior owners as fifty-one percent owners on the record and executing some form of "side deal" which then removes the major incidents of ownership (control over voting the stock, naming directors, declaring dividends, amending the by-laws, etc.) from them. Forget such maneuvers for two major reasons. First, it is illegal, and the I.R.S. tends to get very agitated when it discovers that someone has falsely reported a transaction in order to avoid a tax event. Extremely unpleasant consequences may result, in addition to losing the n.o.l. Second, since the corporate records would not reflect the new, true majority owner, that party would be at the mercy of the (technical) co-owners, who may decide to retake control of the company. If the hidden majority owner then files suit to enforce his rights contained in the side agreement, he may find the court unsympathetic and face the prospect of incriminating himself.

In spite of everything just said about the n.o.l., undoubtedly you will do handstands to try and retain it. Good luck! The best suggestion for preserving the n.o.l. is to consider becoming a minority shareholder and sharing control with the present owners, in a situation where you feel that they have valuable skills to contribute and that you can work well with them. That is, become an investor. (See Chapter 12.)

Some assets are even more intangible in that they do not show up on the balance sheet or profit/loss statement at all. As your investigation of the company proceeds, you should attempt to ferret out the existence of any such assets.

You will want to review sales contracts and firm orders in hand. These may be your most valuable assets because they will prevent a lag in receipts when you take over the business. They also provide an element of predictability for the immediate future, although with any luck you will improve upon that picture.

You should be cautious about existing contracts and orders, because sales do not always equal profits. One common cause of business failure is the inability to properly price the product, as many owners are essentially salespeople who get bored reviewing the financial records in order to determine proper pricing. Many equate sales and production with being successful, until the expenses overwhelm the receipts. Consequently, it is of the utmost importance to determine the *profitability* of current contracts and orders, not only to determine whether they essentially are assets or liabilities, but also to determine what you have to do to operate profitably in the future.

You should determine whether the company has any major claims against other companies or individuals and, if so, analyze them carefully. While usually it is not possible to be certain that a claim will succeed, some calculations should be done, recognizing that most court suits are compromised and settled. The expense of prosecuting a claim is a major factor and may lessen its value. One good strategy is to exclude the Chapter 11 company's claims against third parties from the assets to be purchased when making an offer to buy the business, accomplishing two goals: it places the burden of deciding whether to prosecute the claims upon the creditors, and it leaves them a "sweetener" that may add to their dividend.

A little touchier are the claims that the Chapter 11 company may have that exist only because of the bankruptcy laws. "Preferences" are payments made outside the ordinary course of business to unsecured creditors within ninety days prior to the filing of the bankruptcy petition, and may be reclaimed by the Chapter 11 company even though they were perfectly legal when made. "Fraudulent conveyances" are liens granted or payments made prior to the filing of the bankruptcy for which the Chapter 11 company received no or inadequate consideration therefor. The rules for exercising such rights are very technical, but the point to be made here is that they represent methods for bringing cash into the bankruptcy estate. (See Chapter 7 for more complete discussion.) However, since enforcement of those claims requires the Chapter 11 company to sue its creditors and/or its own executives, the decision to sue may be most difficult. Again, leaving those rights in the estate may constitute a "sweetener" for the creditors and prevent you from getting bogged down in old business.

Chapter 7

Learning the Liabilities

The filing of a bankruptcy creates a "snapshot" of the Debtor's liabilities as they exist on the date of the filing of the bankruptcy petition (the "prepetition debt"). For a Chapter 7 liquidation case, the liabilities are paid from the liquidation of the assets. For a Chapter 11 case, the liabilities are held in abeyance.

While the Chapter 11 Debtor is often required to make some payments upon secured debt, it *cannot* make *any* payments to pre-petition unsecured creditors. So, to a large extent, the debt which has burdened the Debtor is frozen during the Chapter 11 case until a Plan of Reorganization, which must deal with all of the pre-petition debt, is approved.

The debts of a party in bankruptcy are arranged in a hierarchy pursuant to rules set out in the bankruptcy code. In general, not one penny of a debt that is lower in the hierarchy can be paid until the *entire amount* of every debt higher in the hierarchy is paid or all of the higher level creditors approve.

The hierarchy is by "classes" of debts. At the top of the hierarchy are all "secured" debts. Next are "priority" claims. Then come the bulk of the creditors, who hold "unsecured" claims. At the bottom of the pole are the ownership interests.

Secured Debt

At the pinnacle of the creditor hierarchy stands the "secured" claimant. Such a claimant holds a "lien," also known as a "security interest," on a specific asset or assets that then become the "collateral" for payment of the loan. In other words, the creditor has "security" for payment of the debt. The effect of holding a lien is that the creditor may not only be paid out of the Debtor's general funds but, in the event of failure to pay, may take possession of the collateral, hold a sale, and apply the proceeds to the unpaid debt. Liens arise in two ways, either by agreement between the Debtor and creditor or by unilateral action of an unpaid creditor pursuant to law.

You probably are familiar with the situations that commonly give rise to consensual liens. For consumers, a lender usually takes a lien only upon the specific property for which the loan was acquired, whether it be furniture, a car, or a home. (A "mortgage" is simply a lien on real estate.) For a business, the usual circumstance involves a bank which lends working capital and takes a "blanket lien" on all of the company's "personal property" (non-real estate). Another common business situation involves a supplier who will sell on credit only if it receives a security interest in its shipments. Sometimes a debtor will give a lien to a persistent trade creditor after the fact. Essential elements of these types of liens are that they are created by *voluntary agreement* of the parties, and the subject of the lien, the collateral, is designated by them at the time the agreement is made.

If the company or its principal owns its place of business, commonly the real estate is encumbered by one or more mortgages. A lender has probably taken a mortgage to secure the loan given to buy the property. Often a bank that has provided operating loans for the business will take a second mortgage (subordinate to the first mortgage, but a lien nevertheless) on the real estate in addition to a blanket lien on the business assets, under the theory of grabbing as much security as the market will bear. In some states, such as Illinois and Florida, state law allows for "land trusts," and the lien takes the form of an "assignment of beneficial interest" in the trust. The land trust allows the lender to transform what otherwise would be a real estate mortgage into a lien that is similar to that of a lien on personal property, for ease of foreclosure.

A mortgagee of commercial real estate also commonly takes a lien on the rents the property generates, called an "assignment of rents." However, if the lender does not take action to collect rents before the filing of the bankruptcy petition, it becomes barred once the Chapter 11 case is commenced.

An involuntary lien arises when the Debtor has failed to pay an obligation, and the creditor takes steps laid out by statute to change the claim from merely one for money payment to one which attaches to certain property of the Debtor.

This often occurs when the unsecured trade creditor or unsecured lender acquires a judgment against the Debtor. In most states the judgment itself does nothing more than determine the existence and fix the amount of the debt. However, the judgment creditor may then take steps (which vary from state to state) to improve its position through the imposition of a judicial lien upon the Debtor's assets. Again following state statutes, it may then move to foreclose upon the assets.

A few types of creditors have gained a special status through statutes and may impose liens without first obtaining a judgment. The leading example is Uncle Sam—the Internal Revenue Service can slap a lien on you simply by following its own administrative procedures. Another common example is the "mechanics' lien," which was created to ensure payment to the tradesman by allowing him to establish a lien on the specific property upon which he worked, by filing a notice. By state laws, real estate taxes are automatically liens on the subject property.

Formalities must be strictly followed. In the case of consensual liens, the debtor must sign a written "security agreement" (for real estate, a "mortgage") that states specifically which items of property—or classes of property, such as "inventory"—form the collateral. In order to be enforceable ahead of third parties' claims, a lien must then be registered with the correct government office(s). (State laws vary on where different types of liens must be filed.) Generally, a lien that is not properly registered becomes unenforceable in bankruptcy and drops down to the status of an unsecured claim.

Strictly speaking, secured creditors do not form one "class." Each secured claim is considered unique and is related only to the asset or assets that form the collateral. If several creditors have liens on an asset, the lien that was imposed first must be paid in full before the next following lien can start receiving the proceeds from sale of the asset.

In fairness to the unsecured creditors, the bankruptcy code provides that any lien that is taken for a previously existing debt that is acquired within ninety days of the filing of the bankruptcy petition, is voidable by the Debtor. The time period is extended to one year for such a lien taken by an "insider," such as the owner of the Debtor. The claim then becomes unsecured.

Because the secured creditor has placed itself in a position where it may look to specific property for payment, any Chapter 11 Plan of Reorganization must propose to pay the secured creditor no less than the value of the security, by either turning over the collateral to the secured creditor, paying the secured creditor the value of the collateral in cash, or paying the secured creditor in installments with interest. If the value of the collateral is not sufficient to support full payment to the secured creditor, the remainder of the claim is considered to be unsecured.

In general, the secured creditor is in a rather strong position, whether before or during a debtor's bankruptcy case. A Chapter 11 filing will prevent foreclosure, but sooner or later the creditor's secured claim must be honored.

"Priority" Claims

Certain unsecured claims against the Debtor are given a "priority" status by the bankruptcy code, in that they must be paid in full prior to the unsecured creditors receiving anything. Priority status is awarded for policy reasons, and the claimant need not follow any formalities to achieve that status. In general, tax claims and expenses incurred during the course of the bankruptcy case have priority status.

So as not to encourage the filing of bankruptcy to wipe out obligations to the government, most types of taxes are included in the priority category. Priority taxes include those based on income, gross receipts, withholding, and excise, as well as any related compensatory penalties. Through some rather complicated bankruptcy code provisions, certain stale tax claims are not awarded priority status and may be treated as unsecured claims. However, it is rare for the government to allow taxes to remain unpaid for very long without the imposition of a lien, and so usually one can assume that unpaid taxes that do not show as liens must be paid on a priority basis.

In fact, the management of the Chapter 11 company may be quite insistent that the priority status of tax debts *not* be challenged. For a number of types of taxes—most notably, employee income and social security taxes required to be withheld by the employer—the individuals in charge for the employer acquire *personal* liability for the amount of the unpaid taxes. If priority status is successfully challenged, the tax debt drops to unsecured status and most likely will not be paid in full even through a successful reorganization of the company. Since the executives would then have to make up the difference, seeing to it that the company pays these taxes is a primary motivation of an owner in a Chapter 11 reorganization.

While Congress felt it important to prevent the avoidance of tax liability through bankruptcy, it softened the impact somewhat. A provision in the code gives the Chapter 11 Debtor the right, not subject to objection by the government, to take up to six years after the date of assessment of the tax to pay a priority tax claim if payment is made pursuant to a Plan of Reorganization. The Debtor must pay interest on what becomes, in effect, a government loan.

The provision has proven very important as *no similar statutory relief from the requirement of immediate payment of taxes exists outside of bankruptcy.* It has proven very effective in granting a "new lease on life" to companies where management has used tax dollars to attempt to sustain operations, when otherwise the size of the tax liability might preclude reorganization. While few companies file a Chapter 11 proceeding just to spread out their tax liabilities—usually unpaid taxes are a symptom of larger creditor problems—tax relief becomes a nice added bonus for filing.

Also accorded a priority over unsecured creditors are the expenses incurred during the Chapter 11 in operating the business and administering the bankruptcy case, commonly referred to as "costs of administration."

Thus trade debts that arose during the bankruptcy case and are unpaid at the time a Plan of Reorganization is approved, must be paid in full through the plan. If the Debtor has borrowed money (upon prior court approval only), any such loans have priority status.

Fees incurred to professionals during the case also have priority status. The Debtor's accountants and lawyers must be paid fully through any Plan of Reorganization. If the Unsecured Creditors' Committee has retained lawyers and/or accountants, the Debtor must pay those also—sort of like a divorce.

Other miscellaneous unpaid costs of administering the bankruptcy case must also be paid by the Debtor in full. Foremost among these is the monthly fee recently instituted to pay for the U.S. Trustee program. The fee varies with the amount of the Chapter 11 company's assets. Other court costs, such as for transcripts of proceedings ordered by the Debtor, also must be paid in full.

There are certain other statutory priorities, which usually are not major problems: wages, up to two thousand dollars per person, earned within ninety days prior to the bankruptcy; employee benefits up to two thousand dollars per person, accruing within 180 days prior to the bankruptcy; consumer deposits with the Debtor for goods or services, up to nine hundred dollars each; debts of the company arising between the filing of an involuntary bankruptcy petition against it and the date on which the court approves the petition; and grain producers or fishermen, up to two thousand dollars each (thanks to certain powerful senators).

Ordinarily, costs of administration are not overwhelming, but sometimes they can get out of hand. That situation occurs when the case has been open for some time, and the company's operations have been insufficient to support the carrying costs. Perhaps actions by creditors have provoked fights that have driven up the Debtor's attorneys fees. Sometimes the Debtor has been allowed to continue operations in the face of mounting accounts payable. At some point the cost of extricating the company from the grasp of Chapter 11 becomes so large, it kills any chance for reorganization.

Unsecured Debt

The unsecured creditors are the "teeming masses" of bankruptcy. Usually they far outnumber the other creditors and may hold claims that in the aggregate exceed the secured creditors' claims. However, they have no claim to any specific assets of the Debtor and can achieve a distribution in bankruptcy only if and when the secured and priority claims are satisfied.

Basically, unsecured creditors are those whose pre-petition claims do not fall into the secured or priority categories. The bulk are those suppliers of goods or services who sold on open account. There may also be lenders, usually friends or family of the owner, who have made unsecured loans. The owner may find himself in this category due to loans (as opposed to capital contributions) that he has made to the company.

Judgment creditors are in no different class than creditors whose claims have not been determined by a court. The judgment creditor is simply one of the masses. The only advantage of a judgment creditor is that the validity and amount of the claim is considered decided and cannot be challenged in the bankruptcy proceeding.

Also in the unsecured category are "contingent liabilities," which are debts the Debtor cannot be sure it has. Perhaps a visitor was injured on company property, but no suit has been instituted yet. Perhaps the company has traded nasty letters with a supplier over a rejected shipment. Even if management believes that there is no liability, the well-advised Debtor will schedule all such contingent liabilities as unsecured debt and litigate the matters in bankruptcy court.

The unsecured creditors' problem lies in the unescapable fact that liquidation value almost never equals book value.

In the event that the Chapter 11 case fails and the company is liquidated, rarely will the forced sale of the assets bring more than a small fraction of their book value. The result in the vast majority of cases is that the claims of creditors far exceed the cash available for distribution to them, especially since the costs of the liquidation first must be paid in full. Thus, rarely do unsecured creditors get more than a few pennies on the dollar upon liquidation, and frequently they receive nothing.

As a result, the unsecured creditors usually will accept a small fraction of their claims through a Plan of Reorganization rather than take their chances on a distribution after liquidation of the Debtor. Therefore, it is within the unsecured creditor group that the purchaser or investor gains the greatest leverage for his dollar.

The Owner's Interest

The bankruptcy code refers to one class of interests as "equity security holders." This includes holders of all types of stock as well as debentureholders. For our purposes we will be concerned with the shareholder, who is the owner of the company.

In the broadest sense of the word, a shareholder is a "creditor," since he has paid money to the company and is entitled to its return upon his surrender of his shares or other evidence of ownership. However, in choosing to be an owner, he is deemed to have voluntarily risked his money to a greater extent than the other creditors. Therefore, the owner as creditor stands at the very bottom of the creditor totem pole in corporate and bankruptcy law.

It is not unusual for the "Shareholder's Equity" line item on the balance sheet of a troubled company to be a minus number, reflecting that liabilities are greater than assets. Such a "negative net worth" means that for all of the owner's capital input, and for all of his blood, toil, tears, and sweat, the company has no book value beyond what the creditors put into it.

The filing of the bankruptcy case brings the subordinated nature of the owner's interest into focus. The unsecured creditors are often resentful that they should be asked to provide large sacrifices so that the owner can retain the company. Although in most cases the creditors do not act on their resentment, there remains a spark that can ignite and result in the owner losing his company to liquidation or unwanted takeover.

The Undebts (Contracts)

Contracts that are in force at the time of the filing of the bankruptcy petition ("executory contracts") are not debts. A contract is executory if *both parties have continuing duties,* whether it be the providing of goods or services or the payment of money. On the other hand, a debt exists when one party has fully performed its part of the bargain and the other then must make payment. Examples of executory contracts include accepted purchase orders under which delivery has not yet been completed, and other ongoing agreements with suppliers and customers. Leases are executory contracts, such as those for the rental of premises, equipment, or vehicles. A very important executory contract is the collective bargaining agreement that binds unionized employees and the company. The bankruptcy rules require that the Debtor file a list of executory contracts along with the Schedules.

While a debt is frozen at the time the Chapter 11 case is filed and must be dealt with in a Plan of Reorganization, the courts will not allow the Debtor to keep the benefit of an ongoing contract while withholding its performance. Accordingly, the Debtor is required to determine whether it will "assume" or "reject" the contract. Further, if the Debtor is to assume the contract, it must cure its past defaults and show the judge that it is not likely to default again in the future.

If the Debtor assumes the contract, for the parties to the contract it is as though the bankruptcy does not exist. Both sides must perform or be in breach. If the Chapter 11 company defaults, the other party may sue and collect ahead of the pre-petition creditors. For example, usually the Debtor wishes to retain its use of premises and equipment and so maintains the leases in effect and continues to make its regular monthly payments under those leases.

Sometimes a particular lease or other contract is onerous to the Debtor; it even may have been a major cause of the bankruptcy. If so, another unique aspect of the bankruptcy law is brought into play, the Debtor's right to reject a contract. Although the rejected party becomes a creditor—the "rejection" is really a breach—the bankruptcy code places the debt that is created into the class of *pre-petition* unsecured creditors. Since the Chapter 11 Debtor will have to pay that creditor only in "discounted" dollars along with the other unsecured creditors, through the bankruptcy law the company has been given the chance to undo a mistake at a low cost.

The bankruptcy code does not place any limitation on the type of contract which may be rejected. For many years after the enactment of the updated bankruptcy code (effective October 1979), no company had the thought, or the nerve, to apply that rule to union contracts. However, in 1986, Continental Airlines, out of corporate desperation and the *chutzpah* of its controlling shareholder, Frank Lorenzo, filed a Chapter 11 case for the express purpose of voiding its burdensome union collective bargaining agreements. The unions argued all the way up to the U.S. Supreme Court that their contracts were somehow different and that the plain language of the code should be limited by the courts. The Supreme Court ruled that Congress did not say in the bankruptcy code that union contracts were exempt from rejection, and so they were not.

Subsequent to the Continental Airlines decision, Congress amended the bankruptcy code at the behest of the unions, but only in compromise form: a Chapter 11 company must now show that its union contracts are so onerous that the company cannot profitably reorganize without their rejection. So, while Congress prevented a wholesale attack on unions through the bankruptcy process, nevertheless in the proper situation the organized employees can be forced to sacrifice for the company's continued existence.

The prospective purchaser or investor should be just as careful in analyzing the executory contracts as in reviewing the debts. He may require the company to reject certain contracts as part of a Plan of Reorganization. If not, he still should know which ongoing obligations he will inherit when he takes over the company.

Debts can be juggled to the Chapter 11 company's advantage.

Things are not always as they seem. Creditors are not always in the category in which they claim to be. Claims can be shifted from one place in the hierarchy to another, in the proper circumstances. Creditors may actually owe money to the Debtor, and so cash can be brought back into the company from creditors. This section will tell you how.

First, a thorough review of the claims may reveal weaknesses. Perhaps a secured creditor has not followed all of the formalities to perfect the lien. Perhaps the tax claim falls outside the time periods described in the bankruptcy code. Such claims drop down to unsecured status, and thus may be greatly compromised through a Plan of Reorganization.

The code provides that a creditor who was preferred by the Debtor in certain ways described below must give up the "preference" and return to the place in the creditor hierarchy in which it would have been. The creditor's sin is that it improved its position within a short time prior to the filing of the bankruptcy, even if its improvement—taking a lien, or receiving payment on its debt—was perfectly legal and morally free of blame. In this way the bankruptcy law provides a modicum of parity among creditors.

A secured claim may be demoted to an unsecured claim if it was acquired as a "preference." The bankruptcy code provides that a lien acquired within ninety days prior to the filing of the bankruptcy that is not based upon a contemporaneous loan or sale on credit, is a preference. For example, liens acquired by judgment and liens given as a palliative to a long-suffering creditor within that period are preferences, while a lien given at the same time a loan is being made cannot be a preference (up to the amount of that loan). Thus a preferential lien can be objected to and the judge can rule that the creditor has only an unsecured claim.

As part of the theory that owners should bear greater risk, the bankruptcy code also provides that the preference period for a lien taken by an owner or other "insider" that is not based upon a contemporaneous loan or sale on credit is *one year.* Thus the poor owner who has taken his lien as an afterthought gets hit with a double whammy: not only has he poured perfectly legitimate loans into the company, but his claim becomes one of the "pack" and therefore unlikely to achieve substantial repayment.

Another type of preference is the payment to a creditor or other transfer of assets within ninety days prior to the filing of the bankruptcy petition on an already existing debt, while the debtor was insolvent, if it allows a creditor to acquire a larger percentage than it would have from the debtor's liquidation. The common situation involves the payment to a supplier who has sold goods or services on credit. Note that a preference does *not* arise if there is no intention to sell on credit; that is, if the supplier takes payment in full at the time of delivery of the goods or services.

This basic preference concept was considered too harsh on innocent trade creditors, and so in 1984 the law was amended to provide that what would otherwise be a preference payment need not be returned if the debt was incurred and the payment made in the ordinary course of both the debtor's and creditor's business. The change has, of course, generated significant litigation and the ins and outs cannot be discussed here. For our purposes it can be said that modest payments made according to standard terms may pass muster, but unsecured creditors who were favored with unusually large payments within ninety days of the filing of the bankruptcy may be required to refund them.

As with the lien preference, there are harsher rules for a preference payment to an "insider" because it is assumed that such a person has more intimate knowledge of the Debtor's finances and more ability to control payments than an outsider. The preference period for a payment to an insider is *one year,* if the other elements can be proven.

(Preference law is one of those bankruptcy subjects that cannot be competently discussed in ten thousand words or less, and so the reader is especially cautioned here that the foregoing amounts to only a practical overview and that an experienced bankruptcy attorney should be employed before making determinations of whether preference suits should be instituted.)

The outcome of a successful suit against a party who has received a preferential payment is that the payment is returned to the Debtor, and the party acquires a pre-petition unsecured claim against the Debtor in the amount repaid. The net result is a very handsome return to the Chapter 11 company which receives back cash at one-hundred-cents-on-the-dollar for use in operations or to help fund a Plan of Reorganization, and yet it needs only to repay that creditor through the plan at, perhaps, pennies-on-the-dollar.

The main problem for the Debtor with preference suits is that they are divisive. The Chapter 11 company finds itself fighting the very parties who hold votes on the company's future. Consequently, it is the rare (and desperate) Chapter 11 company that rushes to initiate preference suits, and the prospective investor or purchaser may be unable to get an accurate fix on the nature and extent of the claims. However, the Debtor can be required to institute and complete preference actions as a precondition for investment. Sometimes even the investor does not wish to stir up the hornets' nest, and he agrees with management that the best time to challenge claims and institute preference actions is after the Plan of Reorganization has been approved, which is allowed by the bankruptcy code.

Rejection of contracts can also alter the picture. Again the effect is on *net,* as the cancellation of a contract produces a claim on the part of the other party that is treated as a pre-petition unsecured claim. However, where the contract has proven to be most unwise, relief can provide a large boost to the Debtor.

Verify and Determine the Obligations

Now that you have received the short course in "Obligations Under the Bankruptcy Code," you can proceed to investigate the liabilities of potential target companies. A good way to start is to review each company's court records.

The first reference should be Schedule A of the Debtor's "Schedules of Assets and Liabilities," which lists the liabilities by categories: Priority (A-1); Secured (A-2); and Unsecured (A-3). It is usually helpful to make a photocopy of the listed debts.

Some words of caution mentioned elsewhere in this book should be repeated here. While Schedule A provides the initial reference point, unfortunately it is the rare company for which the listed debts are the final word. There is a high correlation between troubled companies and poor record keeping, and for many Chapter 11 companies, scheduling the debts is a hit-and-miss proposition. Sometimes the schedules turn out to be mere figments of the owner's imagination, which should provide a warning "red flag" to you. It is also common for troubled companies to be embroiled in disputes with suppliers and/ or liability suits with customers that have wide-ranging potential outcomes. Consequently, a thorough review of a Chapter 11 company's obligations will quickly move beyond the schedules.

As your interest in a company continues, remember to recheck those important sources of information, the claims docket and filed claims, because additional claims can be filed up to and including the "bar date," the deadline set by the bankruptcy judge. If the bar date has passed, you know your review most likely has encompassed all of the potential prepetition claims.

The court file may disclose that the Debtor has objected to a claim. If the bankruptcy judge has not ruled on the objection yet, the pleadings in the court file may give you a feeling for the issues and the likely outcome. However, commonly the Debtor avoids antagonizing creditors and does not file objections until after a Plan of Reorganization is approved.

Unfortunately, a possible result of your investigation up to this stage is a feeling that you do not really know the total liabilities of the company within a reasonable range of accuracy, and so you should take further steps to attempt to pin them down. You can telephone the Debtor and the creditors to prove the reliability of the schedules and the claims. You can ask for copies of contracts, leases, and other documents. With a cooperative Debtor, or because of pressure on your behalf from creditors, the Debtor may allow you to review its ledger books and other financial records directly. Of course, at an early stage in your investigation you may not wish to make yourself known in such a manner, and so you may have to content yourself with a general knowledge of the liabilities and a general feeling about the reliability of the schedules.

At later stages, when your interest is well known, you may wish to impose conditions upon your continued involvement. You may ask the Debtor to acquire a bar date from the court, if it has not already done so. You may want the court to value the collateral of a pesky secured creditor or to determine the validity and amount of a contingent liability. Although you risk antagonizing some parties, you may ask the Debtor to recover major preferences, challenge the status of certain debts, and/or object to major disputed claims. Such actions may be necessary for you to determine the cost of acquiring the company. (Although, there are ways to finesse such issues, such as providing a flat sum to be shared by the unsecured creditors—however much their claims may turn out to be—rather than providing for a fixed percentage payment of each such debt. Providing for a flat sum puts the onus on the creditors to police their own.)

Another element of your review is to decide the contracts and leases that the company should retain and those that should be rejected which will affect the mix of pre-petition debts and ongoing obligations.

Look for Hidden Liabilities and Costs

Already in this book you have been warned that inaccurate book-keeping and willful or unintentional misstating of debts on both the creditor and Debtor sides can hinder determination of liabilities. You should also guard against major claims that may not appear in the court file at all.

Hidden liabilities pose a severe threat. If a potential claimant is not aware of the bankruptcy case and makes a claim after the company has been reorganized, that party is *not* bound by the Plan of Reorganization and can require payment in full. Thus it is imperative that potential claimants be identified, listed in the Schedules (through amendment, if necessary), and provided notice of the bankruptcy case. The general rule among bankruptcy lawyers is "When in doubt, list them," but sometimes Debtors do not adequately inform their lawyers. The prospective investor or purchaser should always remain sensitive to clues respecting hidden liabilities.

The first category of hidden liabilities involves unlisted contract claims. Are there trade creditors whom the Debtor has neglected to place in the Schedules? Have any purchasers cancelled any orders due to the Debtor's failure to deliver? Has the Debtor had problems manufacturing to its or customers' specifications? Has anyone complained that the Debtor's product or service has caused damage or disrupted operations, even if no suit has been filed? In short, is there any specific occurrence or operational pattern that has a reasonable chance of providing the foundation for a breach of contract lawsuit against the Chapter 11 company? Also in this category are possible claims by former executives or shareholders who were forced out prior to the bankruptcy.

The second category concerns claims for personal injuries that have not yet been made in a lawsuit. Are the company's products of a type that have a measurable risk of producing injury? Have there been any recent accidents on the premises or involving company vehicles? Of course, all or a portion of those claims may very well be covered by the company's insurance, but you should verify coverage. (Beware of a company that has not carried liability insurance at any time in the last five years.)

At some point your accountant should investigate the manner in which the company has performed its tax obligations. Some owners have rather "creative" views of the tax laws that could result in additional taxes, interest, and penalties being imposed upon the corporation at some later date, perhaps after an audit. The taxing body may not be barred from asking for additional sums, even if it was seemingly paid in full through the reorganization. It is exceedingly bad form for an outsider to require the owner to request I.R.S. tax audits to verify its books and records, so the prospective purchaser or investor must rely on his accountants for an opinion.

A new and deadly time bomb consists of environmental claims— governmental rights to require the clean-up of polluted areas. Under many states' laws, as well as federal statutes, it is not necessary for the government to prove intent or negligence to impose liability. A property owner may be required to remove toxic waste even if that owner did not put it there. Perfectly legal users of a perfectly legal waste disposal site may be required to pay for the removal of all waste if the federal government declares it to be a "Superfund" site. Such claims can be made many years after the pollution was created.

The devastating feature of environmental claims is their size. Removing even a modest amount of polluted material or toxic waste can be extremely costly, out of proportion to a company's normal disposal costs. Because the site most likely has years' worth of deposits, clean-up may require removal of large amounts of material and possibly incineration. Usually the extent and ultimate cost of a clean-up project cannot be determined at the onset. Since insurance generally does not pay for clean-up costs, an environmental claim by a government agency can spell the demise for a company.

Another problem with environmental claims is that they are favored in bankruptcy over other types. Recently, courts have ruled that environmental claims made during the bankruptcy—i.e., the government requests that the company be required to fund a clean-up which is not completed prior to the filing of the bankruptcy—are priority "cost of administration" claims regardless of when the pollution was created. Accordingly, they cannot be paid with discounted dollars as pre-petition unsecured claims and can destroy any chance for reorganization.

As a result of all these factors, it is unwise to consider purchasing or investing in a company that may face environmental claims in the future. These claims could be far beyond the company's capacity to pay.

In addition to hidden liabilities, the prospective investor or purchaser should be on the lookout for future *increases* in the cost of doing business. Will leases and other contractual arrangements be terminating within the next year? Does the present owner enjoy some special relationship that may end soon or be terminated if you take over—for example, do his family members provide goods or services at reduced prices? Is the company now paying reduced rent because the company owner also owns the premises? Does your investigation disclose that the present owner is cutting corners in a fashion that you will not?

You may create additional future expenditures through moving to different premises, obtaining additional equipment, and/or incurring other expansion costs. Do not forget to include such added costs of doing business into your projections.

Chapter 8

Do You Want It?

When considering purchasing or investing in a Chapter 11 company, the most important thing you can know is what caused the company to file the bankruptcy petition. If you know that, you know whether making it profitable is within your capabilities.

While this book is not devoted to the nonbankruptcy aspects of purchasing a business, from my vantage point in bankruptcy court, I do have some observations about general economic factors that are very strong influences in determining the success or failure of businesses and that should be addressed when investigating a target company. Of course it is possible to do well even in very adverse situations through ingenuity and perseverance, but it is easier to do well–and possible to do "more well"–when conditions exterior to the business are favorable. Consequently, you might wish to add the following concerns to your analysis of target companies.

Your first task is to determine whether *outside forces* have created conditions that make it impossible to make a profit.

The most important outside force in todays markets is foreign manufacture. There are numerous products that absolutely cannot be manufactured in the United States today, products on which the United States had a lock just a few years back. Why? The iron laws of economics dictate that products manufactured in a country with the lowest manufacturing costs have a comparative advantage over those manufactured in other countries.

There is no point in trying to fight if you cannot come close to matching foreign competitors' manufacturing costs, unless:

1. either the target company or you have offshore manufacturing capabilities that will allow you to compete effectively;

2. the target company has some protected niche; or
3. the industry's economic advantages of manufacturing outside the U.S. are eroding.

The third exception is most intriguing. Many U. S. business people have a growing optimism that they can compete with Japan, Inc., up-and-coming Korea, Inc., etc., because of the disciplines already forced upon American manufacturers by their foreign competitors. Another factor is that many customers have learned that a cheap price may not be worth the aggravation in dealing with companies that make the product a world away, and they are willing to buy from U. S. manufacturers if given half a chance (i.e., if the quality and reliability are there).

Aside from foreign competition, the competitive picture within the United States must be addressed. If the industry is overly concentrated (only a few competitors), you must be sure that you have a deep enough pocket to meet their attempts to drive you out of business. If you have staying power, owning a business in such an oligopolistic market can be quite profitable. If the industry has excess competition, most certainly it is not possible to make a profit in the near future and, ultimately, there will be a big shake-out.

Recently I represented a commercial baking company in its Chapter 11 case and got involved helping the owner in his attempts to sell the company. At first I was quite enthused, believing that the business only needed a better management team to make it profitable. However, I began to notice that quite a few such companies were in Chapter 11 in my district, and I began to feel that the industry itself was under duress for some reason that I did not understand. The company was eventually sold to a close competitor that wanted to add its routes—it simply was not worth the risk for any outsider to the industry to purchase it.

Another important influence outside the immediate product market is the federal government. Profitability in many industries depends upon certain tax, fiscal, or tariff policies. State and local regulations are becoming increasingly more costly. Protection of our planet and its population is going to be costing some industries more than they can afford to pay. Many good businesses and good business people have been crushed by the tide of economic forces unleased or redirected by governmental action.

The effects of a number of such actions have been played out in bankrupcy court. The Carter twenty percent interest rates put the banks in the loan-sharking business alongside the Mafia for a while. Who could make a profit and meet the interest payments? The early Reagan years saw a tight-credit depression. The 1987 real estate bust was triggered by changes in the tax laws.

The practical problem is obvious—predicting governmental trends is a tricky business. However, you should attempt it as best as you can.

While I do not believe that it is determinative, general economic conditions must also be considered. There are better and worse times to start a business. There are better and worse times to enter a particular industry. General economic conditions affect the ease with which loans may be obtained and the patience of bankers. It is easier to sell to people who think things are rosy than to those who are preparing for a recession. However, many things may overrule the adverse effect of poor general economic conditions, such as the presence of a unique opportunity, the right price, etc.

Presence of any of the above negative factors, singly or in tandem, can create a situation for your target company where it simply is not possible for it to make a profit in the foreseeable future. If so, you should know it and either bide your time, allow for near-term losses in return for establishing a position in the market, shift your search to another industry, or develop a specific, unique strategy for success with the target company. If none of the aforementioned outside forces are dominant, than the failure of the owner/managers of the Chapter 11 company to obtain profitability is the result of their inadequacy. Your next step is to determine whether you can fill the gap(s).

Generally speaking, if there are no dominant negative external factors, then the primary cause of bankruptcy for small businesses is lack of adequate capital. The capital requirements of some industries can be very substantial, but most undercapitalization situations result from attempting to operate "on a shoestring."

Many people entering into business do not have, or allocate, enough capital to the business to give it staying power. They provide only the bare minimum to capital reserves, often the least that the state will allow when a business incorporates (e.g., one thousand dollars in Illinois). Thinly capitalized companies are only as strong as this month's receipts—they have no ability to bounce back from a run of bad luck or bad decisions. Also, they have no extra resources to take advantage of opportunities for increased sales or lower costs.

The bookkeeping result of thin capitalization is, of course, an astronomical "debt-to-equity ratio," a common standard of measuring a company's financial health. (Business administration texts say that a healthy ratio is less than 1:1, a number I almost never see in small companies, even in my nonbankruptcy corporate clients!) Banks do not encourage high debt-to-equity ratios. At very high ratios, the bank considers itself to have more at risk than the owner and thus in effect to be a venture partner, and banks do not like to be venture capitalists. That is the major reason why small businesses have such trouble acquiring bank financing.

A secondary problem is that the relatively high bank debt makes the business very sensitive to rises in interest rates. Business bankruptcy filings go up with the interest rates.

If thin capitalization is the number one culprit, you should not fall prey to it. Make a dollar-for-dollar determination of your capital requirements—initially, and on a flow chart—which allows for slower than expected start-up time, production snafus, bad receivables, and so on. Pinpoint the primary problem with the business and make specific plans to solve it quickly. If your wallet is too thin, recognize that you have an increased risk of replicating the company's Chapter 11 case.

One type of thin capitalization situation that is encountered with some frequency in bankruptcy may provide the best investment/ purchase opportunity: the mature company that has been milked as a "cash cow" and now has insufficient reserves to weather a mistake or market change. The problem is seen mostly in small but successful family-owned businesses. The "old man" built it up through hard work, but the sons, daughters, their children, and other relations view it as a money machine which runs itself. Excess funds are quickly siphoned off, and innovation (read: proposals to spend money now for future profits) is stifled. When the business suffers a setback, whether through neglect, paralysis, or active mismanagement, it may need bankruptcy court relief from creditors. While it is usually the controlling management that puts the company into Chapter 11, sometimes it is the minority faction, which feels (a) hurt, (b) outvoted, (c) that it can do a better job, or (d) all of the above, that forces a Chapter 11 filing.

Once ensconced in the protective arms of the bankruptcy court, the family factions quickly find that they cannot cooperate to solve their problems. They also fear harm to their standard of living if the company is liquidated and the bank calls in the family members' guarantees. The banker, who has been virtually a friend of the family for all these years, turns unfriendly. Very often the factions start looking for an outside investor or purchaser.

The thinly capitalized mature business offers advantages and disadvantages, of which most are related to its established position in the industry. Negatively, it may be in a mature industry that suffers from overcompetition or is declining due to changes in economic conditions. It may need massive funds to modernize its equipment and/or operating methods. On the other hand, it may have a product that is well established in the marketplace. It may have a solid base of customers and (still) much goodwill with its suppliers. It may offer solid advantages over starting from scratch and attempting to crack a market.

When coupled with a cash-poor situation, management inadequacies produce more severe consequences than when the company has some financial leeway. In some cases, the executives are totally incompetent or obviously inattentive, and a series of self-imposed crises forces the company into Chapter 11. More often it is more subtle than that. The owners and executives may seem reasonable and competent, but close scrutiny reveals a "blind spot" that causes the downfall.

Every once and a while, there is *staggering* management incompetence. I recently located an assembly operation in Chapter 11 that had severe production problems. It soon became clear that the cause was the owner, who created horrendous labor problems through his inability to deal with his employees and had not the faintest idea how to get a product out the door. (The interesting thing is that he had a graduate degree in business from a very prestigious—but very theoretical— university.) The owner was tired of the battle and wished to sell out.

I lined up a group that was interested in taking a look at the company and set up an appointment with the owner. Much to my amazement and embarrassment, when we arrived at the plant for the meeting we learned that operations had been suspended in a fit of pique by the owner as a result of an argument with his foreman the workday before. As a result of his choosing to lay off all of his production force the day before our meeting (!), it was not possible to see the company in operation. Because my clients did not want to undertake to restart operations, and because they were not able to view the production lines, the meeting quickly terminated.

As if that blunder were not enough, after I located another group that expressed an interest even under these adverse conditions, I then learned that the owner had called all of his major customers, cancelled their contracts, and told them to buy elsewhere even as he was attempting to sell his company. Of course, the company was then closed permanently and the assets sold at auction, much to the loss of the owner (who had personally guaranteed much of the debt). I never could figure out why the owner was so incredibly self-destructive.

Often there is thin management, especially in single-owner companies. The owner may be too busy flying around the country making sales to scrutinize the expense ledger; or the inventor-owner does not know how to build sales. Many of the most successful small companies are owned by two relatively equal partners: a "Mr. Inside" who oversees production and loves poring over the books, and a "Mr. Outside" who is the gregarious salesman and goodwill ambassador to the outside world. They may hate each other, but they make a winning team.

Sometimes the prospective purchaser realizes that the cause of unprofitability is theft. If it has been by lower echelon employees, the situation can be corrected by better controls. If it has been by the owners, and/or if the books show evidence of being "crooked" regularly, it is not possible to know what problems will surface in the future and the company should be avoided.

Of course there is always The Big Mistake. The company may have intentionally or unintentionally bet all its marbles on a big contract or new product that failed miserably. Overexpansion, or overspending on expansion, is an endemic problem. The company may have been hit by some production or quality problem, such as a strike or sudden plunge in market acceptance. These types of companies also offer fertile grounds for purchase or investment because the problems are correctable by astute management.

Besides searching for the causes of the company's troubles, you should take some care to look for the kernels of gold. The main goal is to focus on the factors that will fuel the acceleration of momentum and profitability.

What are the positive aspects of the company's operations? Perhaps a segment of the business is doing a good job, either making the sales or getting the product out the door. The business may have substantial goodwill with customers. Try to spot the key employees who are assets to the company. It is helpful to note the things that will *not* have to be changed, as well as the things that will. Very few companies in Chapter 11 for any period of time are totally and hopelessly messed up—those companies sink quickly and are liquidated.

What is there about this particular company that intrigues you, that keeps your mind working on the bits and pieces of its situation? You may find the product line to be really interesting, generating all kinds of thoughts about how you could market it. The company's technology may provide a solid base for products that you feel you could develop. Perhaps the company has already established a spot in an industry that is growing or is otherwise desirable. There might be a multiplier effect to the positive elements, if you realize that they have greater value than others are allocating to them. The result will be the acquisition of valuable assets at a very favorable price.

The best "good news" probably is the growing feeling that you can take that creaky company and fine tune it, that you can really make it hum. You may be gaining confidence that you can coordinate those parts working at odds to each other and harness the power which can be produced. If so, that company has much to offer you.

Having identified the strong points and problem areas of the target Chapter 11 company and having decided that its problems are manageable, you should consider the "Critical Path" that you will take to produce a turnaround in the event that you assume control of the company. (According to R. Buckminster Fuller,* the Critical Path for accomplishing a complex task is a listing, in chronological order, of the specific actions that must be taken to achieve the task in the most efficient manner.) The advantage of determining the Critical Path is that it not only delineates the specific actions required, but also highlights the order in which they must be done and *when the assets necessary to do them must be marshalled.*

No doubt important and far reaching changes in operations will be made once you arrive on the scene. As it is not possible to undertake all those tasks at once, and complete them instantaneously, when and how they are to be accomplished should be part of your Critical Path. For example, you might hire a new sales manager and create updated product brochures during your first month, and then tackle production problems as increasing orders come in. Complex tasks, such as reorganizing operations, make take a substantial period of time and may be made up of a number of specific tasks that should be added to the Critical Path.

A companion to the "Critical Path" is a determination of the cash requirements of the business for the foreseeable future. In effect, profit/

---

*R. Buckminster Fuller, *Critical Path* (New York: St. Martin's Press, 1981).

loss statements are projected, and if the bottom lines are positive, no additional cash input will be required—but if they are negative, additional cash will have to be devoted to operations, either through the owners' capital contributions or loans or through outside financing. Most such cash flow projections are done on a spread sheet that covers twelve consecutive months going forward. However, there may be situations that require weekly, or even daily, projections.

While the cash flow projection is an important tool for any business, it is doubly important in the bankruptcy takeover situation. Not only does it impose discipline in its creation and provide quantifiable goals, but it acts as a microscope focusing on the details of the substantial financial efforts that will be required to achieve turnaround.

Of course, there is an element of unreality in any projection, since by its nature it must be based upon assumptions of future actions and conditions. Accordingly, sound business theory requires that all assumptions (for example: sales levels, delivery times, collections, etc.) be on the conservative side. It is legitimate to include in the assumptions the effects of the changes that you will institute; however, those effects cannot be too dramatic unless you feel very confident that such extreme results are clearly warranted. You should keep a written list of your assumptions.

Even given the fact that assumptions can be in error, the cash flow projection spread sheet imposes requirements upon you which you must be prepared to fill. Expenditures for replacing and supplementing existing machinery and equipment must be allotted. It is not uncommon for such a listing to show that heavy cash expenditures will be required not only to pay the creditors and costs of bankruptcy administration on or about the date of the confirmation of the Plan of Reorganization, but also to support operations for some time after the emergence from Chapter 11. If the plan calls for spreading out payments to secured, unsecured, and/or priority claimants, immediate cash requirements may be eased, but "cash crunches" may arise on dates in the future when payments become due. (This is especially true if future "balloon payments" are promised. Without specific projections, and the creation of an internal sinking fund, it is too easy to forget about the day of reckoning, which initially seems so far away.)

Another important reason for developing cash flow projections is that they are an important prerequisite for acquiring bank financing. The banker wants to know if you will be "coming back to the well." The banker will be impressed if you maintain cash flow projections even before being required to produce them as part of the loan application.

Of course, cash flow projections should be updated as frequently as possible so that you may recognize and respond to changes in conditions and lessons gained from experience. While initially it may seem to be an unprofitable expenditure of your time to continue to produce and update cash flow projections, you will soon learn how valuable the undertaking is to spotlight trends and problems and to require you to think about the future in a directed fashion.

When calculating cash needs, determine as best you can the cost of taking the company out of a Chapter 11. Generally, the accounts payable incurred during the company's Chapter 11 case can be paid in the ordinary course of future operations, but the company's accountants and attorneys will want their bills brought up to date (especially if you will be replacing them with yours). It is not uncommon for those accrued fees already to be substantial if the Debtor has been barely getting by during the Chapter 11 case. Additional fees will be incurred as those professionals represent the Debtor in negotiations with you and the creditors and prepare and acquire approval of the Plan of Reorganization. (Yes, it does not seem fair for you to pay the Chapter 11 company's lawyers, but if it had money to pay for such things it would not need you!)

Your own acquisition costs should be carefully determined. Your attorneys and accountants will no doubt have to be paid on an hourly rate. You may have a need for other professional help, such as business consultants, industrial engineers, etc. If the company or court case is located out of town, you may have travel-related expenses. As with other issues discussed in this book, the need to predict those costs as closely as possible is more acute when acquiring a company in bankruptcy in order to be sure that the benefits outweigh the detriments.

There will be a constant interplay between the actions taken to effectuate a turnaround and the need for cash. Some changes will require additional funds, but some, such as cost cutting, improved relations with suppliers, etc., will reduce the need for cash. Others will increase receipts from sales. Some actions work both ways. For example, purchases of machinery and equipment will require an initial cash outlay—and monthly payments, if financed—but should lead to increased efficiency and lower operating costs once on line.

The end result of your Critical Path determination and your cash flow projection is your "Business Plan." The business plan is your road map to success. It provides checkpoints along the way to keep you from getting lost. It helps you to know something about the road over which you will be passing next. Modifications of the business plan over time simply create a more accurate road map. It is the only way to travel, business class.

The strongest caution I can offer is to warn you not to underestimate turnaround time. No doubt the company has been sliding for some time, and everyone with whom it deals has altered his transactional patterns. It takes time to alter one's patterns, establish new operational patterns, and make an impression in the marketplace. Of course, if you have chosen wisely, a turnaround should not take years to accomplish—but you should allow for those seemingly endless months between your *actions* and the profitable *reactions*.

Once you have done a business plan, including estimating the costs of acquiring the company and taking it out of Chapter 11, you are in a position to determine whether the assets that you have or are willing to allocate are sufficient to do the job.

The cash flow projection should spotlight not only the gross amount of capital input that is required, but also the timing of its application. You may find that while the company needs $500,000, it may only need $200,000 the first month and $50,000 for the next six months. Conversely, you may find a cash influx "spike" of $500,000 in eight months. The *amount* and the *timing* of the company's requirements cannot exceed your capital availability.

Once again, do not ignore the need for a margin of safety. To say that cash needs should match your capital resources is to assume that you have access to additional funds in the event of miscalculation, change of circumstances, etc. Otherwise you may quickly find yourself as the Capter 11 Debtor.

Nonfinancial forms of investment also must be weighed in the balance. Managing a business ordinarily takes large and time-consuming expenditures of mental and physical energy, as well as a certain amount of talent, and turning around a troubled business must surely more than double those requirements. It is *hard work*. Forget the potential rewards for a while and give some thought to whether you (and your spouse) *can* and *will* do what it takes to reap the benefits. Physical and emotional assets are just as important, and just as scarce, as financial assets.

Your storehouse of experience and expertise should be evaluated in light of the tasks called for. If you are young and inexperienced or the target company is in an industry new to you, extra caution is indicated. You may need an extra margin of safety in terms of financial backing and/or the time allowed for turnaround to counter the fact that many situations on the job will be new to you.

The scarcity of nonfinancial assets must be considered, whether you are moving from "employee" status or you already operate a successful business. While it is clear that the new business owner must take a careful inventory of available assets of all types, the successful entrepreneur should not overlook a related form of personal inventory. The entrepreneur must feel confident that the turnaround process will not take so much of his resources that the Goose that Laid the Golden Egg suffers. He must recognize that large amounts of his workday will be devoted to the new acquisition, which has two consequences. First, he must have staff in place at his base company to take on additional duties completely. Second, he will need *very* competent help at the new company. With any luck, the benefits of savvy will outweigh the detriments of divided resources, but the balance is delicate.

Why make $50,000 when you can make $100,000 for the same effort? That is the underlying concept of the economic theory of "opportunity cost."

Put in terms relevant to this book, investment in the target company should have a good chance of producing a return to you which equals or exceeds your other opportunities. Unless you enjoy putting yourself into nerve-wracking situations just for fun, it is just not worth it to take on a turnaround situation when you can do better by investing your money and time elsewhere.

Of course the calculations are not simple. The increased risk and effort of buying a Chapter 11 company must be balanced against the savings of paying for it at a distressed-company price and thus the increased earnings-to-equity ratio which can result from a turnaround. Another problem is that classic economic theory assumes one hundred percent "mobility"—that is, that one can go anywhere and manage any business and that one has full knowledge of all other available opportunities—and in real life such universality does not exist.

The moral of this section is that, having scoped the nature and extent of the situation, just because you *can* overcome the obstacles does not mean that you necessarily *should* accept the challenge. Review your other opportunities also—past, present, and future.

Make a summary chart of positive, borderline, and negative factors. Include it in your calculations of whether to purchase or invest in a Chapter 11 company.

Factors That Say "Yes"

The Company's Strengths:
  Few competitors
  Equipment is hard to find
  Extensive goodwill
  Niche in market
  Growing industry
  Industry is favored by government programs/policies that seem
      likely to continue
  Competent white-collar staff
  Good production employees
  Good sales organization
  Solid product line

The Company's Manageable Problems:
  Thin capitalization
  Thin or weak management
  "Blind spot" caused decline
  Theft by underlings
  The Big Mistake

Factors That Say "Maybe"

Industry is unfamiliar to you
Company needs modernization/new products
Union
Cannot pinpoint causes of decline, but you feel that your manage-
    ment will produce profits
Company seems better positioned than most to survive a shakeout in
    the industry

Factors That Say "No"

Dying industry
Devastating foreign competition
Excessive number of competitors

Excessive "opportunity cost" (you can do better by applying your talents/capital elsewhere)

Cheaper to start your own company than to save this one

Pattern of theft/false bookkeeping by present owners

Your capital is insufficient or would be stretched too thin

You cannot figure out why the company is unprofitable

Are you an eagle or a chicken? From this book, and other books too no doubt, you have learned the methods of analyzing businesses, making projections, and establishing winning patterns. You have probably imagined scenarios of acquisition and success.

The problem is that, in real life, the proper course of action in any given situation is not so obvious. For every action, in every circumstance, there is a percentage chance of failure. Risk cannot be removed from any human endeavor. The better you learn your lessons, the lower the risk—although it will not disappear entirely. The goal is to be a hardheaded optimist.

Entrepreneurs carefully determine the risks and then proceed. They recognize that there are no guarantees of success and that there can be no success without risk. They appreciate that the potential rewards are worth the risks. They fly high in that atmosphere. They are the eagles.

Many people dream of being entrepreneurs, but will only act when the risk is near zero. In effect, they demand a guaranteed, "can't miss" situation. A large percentage of these people are fugitives from the professions—usually law or accounting—where the standard is perfection. Some are investment advisors, whose standard is *extreme* prudence. Those who retain such attitudes should not purchase a business, much less one in bankruptcy.

So, you must answer "yes" to the following questions. Are you willing and able to work hard to be your own boss and enjoy the fruits of business ownership? Do you have the skills and attitudes that are important to the type of business that you wish to enter? Are you confident that you understand the nature of the target company's business, its problems, and how to solve them? Are your mental, physical, and financial assets sufficient to turn the company around and make it profitable? Are the rewards of taking over the target company worth the risks?

In summary, in trying to decide if you want a particular company, go through the following checklist.

What led the company to Chapter 11?

What is the good news of the company?

Map the path for a turnaround.

Do your assets match the needs?

Determine the opportunity cost—what is here versus what is elsewhere.

Chart the pluses and minuses.

Ask yourself if you are an eagle or a chicken

If you like the answers, GO FOR IT!

Chapter 9

How to Go After It

If you have decided to make a run at the target company, you must have determined that its acquisition is within your financial capabilities. While you may have sufficient capital to fund the projected cash requirements, the far more likely situation is that you will borrow a percentage of the required investment. That is, you will "leverage" your own capital. The percentage you borrow will be related to your resources and your general investment theory, but is not without repercussions.

It is enticing to attempt maximum leveraging, achieving the smallest ratio of your own capital to borrowed funds as is possible. That concept is not unknown; in fact, the more sensational books touting munificent-riches-from-little-or-no-investment generally describe strategies involving extreme leveraging. While they provide wonderful fantasies, their underlying concepts of near-one hundred percent leveraging almost always fail in fact for two practical reasons.

The first failure is at the inception of the plan, for in most situations no one needs someone who cannot or will not commit his own funds. If the prospective purchaser has no money, generally speaking there is a lack of credibility because he usually lacks a "track record" as well. Or, put another way, the world is full of people with great ideas and no money. If the prospective purchaser apparently is successful and refuses to risk capital, it is felt that there is a lack of commitment. The players—the banker, the creditors, the owners—all have learned to shy away from the adventurer who is ready to risk the last dollar...of someone else's money. They most likely are jealous that the proposed purchaser may bear no financial risk, while at the same time legitimately concerned over the quality of the commitment.

To be more specific, sound banking practice requires that a borrower risk a substantial amount of his own assets. To some extent this is done through the requirement of the personal guarantee, but the banker generally wants to see the purchaser make more of a commitment than merely being exposed to a contingent liability.

The second failure arises in the execution. Thinly capitalized companies can succeed if major internal and external forces are favorable, but those companies cannot withstand temporary setbacks or adverse situations. Many companies with financial strength "a mile wide and an inch deep" disappear *quickly* in Chapter 11 before resuscitation efforts can be administered.

Leaving aside *extreme* leveraging, how does the prospective purchaser go about achieving "responsible," if somewhat daring, leveraging? There is always the purchaser's own bank, certainly the first choice if he already enjoys a good banking relationship. An alternative is to approach the Chapter 11 company's lender. Approaching a bank that has no prior relationship with you or the target company most likely is a waste of time in a turnaround situation.

By requesting financing from your bank for the acquisition of a troubled company, essentially you are riding on your own reputation. It is difficult to persuade the banker, a pessimist by nature and training, to base the loan on the company's future prospects. He is far more interested in your personal track record and net worth. If you have shown success in the past, he is unlikely to second guess you. Besides, you might take your business elsewhere!

While your bank probably will be looking to your assets to back the loan, there are elements of the deal that may increase your banker's interest, if you highlight them properly. One positive aspect is the way the balance sheet of the Chapter 11 company will look immediately upon its emergence from bankruptcy—it will be beautiful! It may even show a positive net worth. So, be sure to flash a pro-forma "new company" balance sheet in front of your banker's eyes. Also, if you feel strongly about the upside possibilities, it cannot hurt to sell the "sizzle" a bit.

The Chapter 11 company's banker is already "in the frying pan," so his job is to decide whether establishing a relationship with you will lower the heat or end up burning him. He will not take too great a chance, but he will take a far greater chance than he would if he were not already involved. Generally, the banker will feel that he has made a successful transition if you turn the company around, *or if your takeover merely defers the problems for some indefinite time.*

That is right—in truth the banker's major goal is to terminate The Problem, preferably without the bank having to admit defeat and to take a substantial write-off of its loan. If your involvement results in continuity of the business, The Problem will have gone away (at least for now, at least for him). If you have a modicum of personal credentials so that the banker will not be overly embarrassed supporting you, you have a very good chance of persuading that banker to finance the transition.

The first element of financing concerns the outstanding secured loan to the Chapter 11 company. Of course, the banker has become totally disgusted with the business by the time you arrive on the scene, and the first response to your inquiry no doubt will be that the bank wants to be paid off in full on any takeover. That may also be the second, third, and fourth response too, but I suggest that you ignore it. When the time is right and your offer is firm, the bank will consider other alternatives.

In the meantime, your job is to establish a working relationship with the company's banker. You should impress him with your background and abilities. You should sympathize with his plight, while subliminally programming him with the message that you are his way out. In the meantime, you are learning much about the company from him, although the viewpoint may be skewed by his position way out on the limb. *The banker is the most important person you will be called upon to deal with when negotiating for the takeover of a Chapter 11 company, so treat him accordingly.*

Gradually you should bring the banker around to the position that the bank will stay on the loan, that is, it will rewrite the outstanding note and go back onto some form of installment payment plan. Usually the amount of the rewritten principal balance and the terms of the installment payments are negotiable. Just how negotiable depends on how desperate the banker is.

While it may seem strange that the principal balance, a seemingly fixed sum, can be the subject of negotiations, it is not that unusual for a bank to write down the outstanding principal balance when rewriting a note upon a reorganization. In fact, the write-down can be quite large. If the bank is insisting that all accrued interest and the usual array of outrageous charges be paid in full as the price of renegotiation of the note, one useful tactic is to persuade the bank to add those charges, or some percentage of them, to the principal balance of the new note. The next step is to show the banker just how worthless the collateral is and how much of a beating the bank will take if you walk away, and then to chisel down the principal balance. It may take some brinksmanship, and you must be basing your posture upon a realistic assessment of the bank's situation, but it can be done. Do not fall for the banker's line that the principal balance is non-negotiable.

The other arena of negotiations with the bank involves the terms of the new note. Interest rates and payment terms are usually very negotiable. Since obviously there will be a hiatus until the company can gain momentum again, it is not out of line to ask for a moratorium on interest and/or principal payments. A modified position is to ask for minimal payments initially, to be scaled up over time. Balloon payments are commonly negotiated, but they can be dangerous because they provide a period of illusory profitability followed by a doomsday that usually puts the borrower at the mercy of the bank to "roll it over."

You should work hard to negotiate the best deal with the bank as it is this vulnerability of the bank that creates one of the great advantages of buying a company out of bankruptcy. You should not be shy in the negotiations. Better-than-market loan terms simply are a reflection of your risk and the need of the banker to improve his situation.

While a bank usually will not finance all of your cash needs, if the banker is impressed with the level of your commitment, you may be able to sweeten the rewritten note with an additional loan and/or a line of credit. Additional financial support from the bank is easier to acquire if it is clear that there is some large financial hump over which you must pass or that the additional funding quickly will produce an increase in assets (i.e., the bank's collateral). It is brinksmanship to argue that the deal simply will not work without additional bank funding—the banker may question your seriousness—but it might work.

Another avenue for negotiations involves the issue of the "personal guarantee;" that is, the personal liability that you accept for the bank's loans to the company. In nonbankruptcy situations, it is highly unusual for a bank to make a loan to a privately held company that is not backed by the personal guarantee of the owners. Even in the bankruptcy situation, it is most difficult to avoid personal exposure. However, if you have persuaded the bank that you are the company's only savior and that you are virtually doing the bank a *favor* by turning the business around, you may avoid the personal guarantee.

Short of the bank giving you a pass on a personal guarantee, you may be able to negotiate a cap on your exposure and/or other concessions. For example, the new loan documents may provide that your personal exposure is capped at $50,000 and that the bank must fully exhaust efforts to collect from the borrower corporation before it seeks payment from you.

Other issues respecting the personal guarantee involve whether it is secured and whether there are any written restrictions on the guarantor's ability to transfer major assets during the term of the loan. Generally speaking, guarantees of corporate obligations are unsecured and the guarantor has no restrictions on disposal of assets, and so, especially in the bankruptcy situation, you should strongly resist any such overtures by the bank.

Again, I remind you that the bank is unlikely to give you a "free ride"—i.e., require little or no financial risk on your part—even in dire bankruptcy situations. The business world is littered with self-acclaimed turnaround experts with no money, and the bank is unlikely to be panicked to the point where it hands you the keys based only on your promises. If you come into the case with those expectations, you will immediately lose your credibility. *But,* if you are willing to risk some capital, chances are you can achieve a much sweeter deal from the bank in the turnaround situation then when negotiating an ordinary loan.

You must also negotiate with the unsecured creditors. There are wide variations among cases as to how active and how tough the unsecured creditors are. One case may have no Unsecured Creditors' Committee and no major active unsecured creditors (i.e., total silence from that class of creditors). Another may have a highly organized and vocal committee that is convinced that the unsecured creditors would do well to liquidate the Debtor immediately and leaves no fight unfought to accomplish just that.

While the lack of an Unsecured Creditors' Committee leads to somewhat of a mystery about what unsecured creditors will accept in a Plan of Reorganization, on the whole, the situation favors the purchaser of the company. Lack of creditor involvement indicates apathy and, in bankruptcy court, apathy leads to getting shortchanged. (To me, the analogy of the bankruptcy court is that of the boardinghouse dinner table—almost never is there enough to go around, and thems with quick hands and sharp elbows get better fed while thems that hang back and are willing to take what is left go hungry.) Accordingly, usually you can figure that uninvolved creditors will be unable to oppose even a minimal plan, and most likely will meekly accept whatever crumbs you choose to throw their way.

The existence of an Unsecured Creditors' Committee is not necessarily a serious impediment to your takeover plans. While the committee members will like to feel that they have gained something for the unsecured creditor body through negotiations with you (and so you should set up some "straw men" for them to vanquish), in the end the committee usually will veto only the most outrageous proposals. Remember, because of your extensive investigation of the Debtor, the committee is unlikely to be as informed about it as you are. (The exception involves larger cases where the committee may have retained accounts or other experts to value the assets.)

The Unsecured Creditors' Committee can actually be a great help to you. If the Debtor is not receptive to your overtures, the committee can act as your stalking-horse to acquire information about the Debtor and, in situations described in detail later in this book, propose a Plan of Reorganization that is founded upon the sale of the company to you.

If the committee has retained bankruptcy counsel (not all committees want to introduce that expense into the case), the prospective purchaser's leeway is further reduced, but not necessarily to the extent that he should get discouraged. The committee's attorney will veto excessively "cute" proposals by a prospective buyer and will prevent the unsecured creditors from falling prey to the numerous little tricks and strategies that might otherwise victimize them. However, in the end, it will be the Unsecured Creditors' Committee members—business people—who will decide whether to accept the basic financial proposals contained in the Plan of Reorganization.

In many situations, the attorney for the Unsecured Creditors' Committee can facilitate a takeover by an outsider. If the committee members are unsophisticated, the attorney may introduce them to the cold, hard reality that, for example, five-cents-on-the-dollar through a Plan of Reorganization may be better than zero through liquidation.

Be on the lookout for divisions among the unsecured creditors that might benefit you. The conflicts may have already surfaced or they may be lurking, waiting for you to activate them. One of the most common divisions is that between the trade creditors who wish to do business with the Debtor in the future and those who cannot or will not. Often the once-and-future creditors will accept a lower dividend through the plan if you suggest that they will be receiving orders from the revitalized company. It is not unusual to find that such pivotal creditors are influential on the Unsecured Creditors' Committee and thus may persuade the other creditors to accept your proposal. Other conflicts may arise out of personality clashes, friendship with the company owner, etc. Remember that one strong creditor on your side on the committee is worth ten "in the bush."

In perhaps the majority of cases, you will find the Unsecured Creditors' Committee demoralized and passive, the members tired of the Debtor and tired of expending their time and money fulfilling their duties on the committee. While it may not be immediately obvious, a little probing by you may produce the response: we do not really care what you do, *just get it over with.*

It may be necessary to introduce the owner to reality.

The owner of a Chapter 11 company usually seems like a schizophrenic to prospective purchasers, for good reason. The owner carries the hope that a White Knight will arrive bearing saddlebags filled with cash; further, he would prefer the knight to drop off the cash and ride off into the sunset with nothing more than "thanks" as compensation, as men of chivalry are supposed to do. However, modern business reality indicates that today's knight probably intends to buy the castle at foreclosure and boot out the present occupant! Assuming that the owner lacks the wherewithal to turn around the company, his hopes to retain sole control are at odds with reality.

Even during those lucid periods when the owner is ready to talk about selling the company, his view of its value is usually highly subjective. Although often not articulated, in effect the company is his "baby." Another commonly held view, as already mentioned, is roughly translated as "my million hours of work must be worth a million dollars." The end result is a purchase price off the reality scale.

Certain stratagems can be used by you to minimize conflict while investigating the company. You almost guarantee yourself a better reception if you remember to hold yourself out as a prospective *investor*, thus implying to the owner that he will have a place in the reorganized business. While gathering information, refrain from discussing the details of what your offer may entail.

Another strategy involves introducing the owner to reality in the least confrontational way. You may indicate to the creditors that the owner's price is way out of line and get them to straighten out the owner by reminding them of the horrible things which can occur to their claims in the event of liquidation. Your bankruptcy attorney may suggest to the Debtor's bankruptcy attorney that the owner be provided a dose of reality in the form of sound legal advice. Thus you offer the owner the "carrot" of your possible cash infusion while others provide the "stick."

At some point the owner will realize that your offer will leave him little or nothing. He may be happy just to avoid liquidation of the company and escape extensive personal liability to the bank or the taxing agencies. He may be tired of the particular line of business and ready to move on without a fuss. If he is unhappy and turns uncooperative, by that time you should have acquired all of the information you need and can seek out the creditors to sponsor your purchase of the company.

The elements of the "dance" are well illustrated by a situation in which I was involved as a business broker. The owners of the Chapter 11 company were following a number of their options simultaneously, trying to find an investor who would allow them to maintain effective control while also meeting with prospective purchasers. Thus they were willing to establish contact with my client, a possible buyer of the entire business, while they continued to cultivate an "angel" they had found.

Because of the fluid situation over the course of four months, at times my client would be provided important operating information by the owners and at times would be given the Cold Shoulder. For most of that period that suited my client just fine, since the periods of thaw allowed time to collect sufficient data. In the meantime, it became obvious that the owners could not wrap up their deal with their angel, although they kept trying. All the while the business languished for lack of capital and because the owners lacked the ability to correct the production problems. As the company's situation deteriorated, it became clear that a large capital infusion would be required imminently.

As "doomsday" approached, the owners intensified their efforts to finalize their sweetheart deal and became more difficult to deal with. Accordingly, on several occasions I had the attorney for the Unsecured Creditors' Committee force the Debtor to provide my client with needed information. On each occasion the company's owners were reminded that they had fiduciary duties to the creditors, arising from the Chapter 11 status, to provide information to "all comers" and to make the company available for sale to outsiders. Each time, the company grudgingly did its duty.

While my client initially entertained the idea of working with the owners, it became obvious that the only thing that the owners were interested in was finding someone who would invest a large pile of money and leave their positions, perks, and power in place. Since that was unacceptable to my client, when it came to pass that he made an offer to buy the company, he made it through the Unsecured Creditors' Committee and without the cooperation of the owners.

Unfortunately, because my client had waited—against my advice— to make his offer until the owners had wrapped up their deal with their investor and had made a motion to have that deal approved, he was not able to effectively contest them and failed to acquire the company. Some of the lessons to be learned from that episode hark back to the time of the Bible: there is a time to cooperate, a time to be pushy, a time to bide your time, and a time to move your butt and make an offer! Or something like that.

An assumption of the discussion so far is that your intent is to purchase the company and send the former owner packing. However, at the conclusion of your investigation, you may conclude that an owner offers managerial skills that would greatly aid the road to profitability. Perhaps his skills complement yours and would help make the company formidable. As you finalize your plans, perhaps you should rethink your initial idea to go it alone.

If you feel that the chemistry is right, you may decide to offer the owner a "partnership" (even if it is in corporate form) in return for an additional contribution of capital. If you decide to go that route, it is likely your path to ownership will be greatly smoothed.

Having sufficiently negotiated with the owners and the creditors to understand the reasonable range of their interests, it is time to make a formal offer. The offer should be definitive and should indicate the manner and the extent to which each interest will receive compensation. The offer should lay the foundation for the Plan of Reorganization.

Too often outsiders with a genuine interest squander their credibility by making tentative or incomplete offers, leaving the parties to wonder what the acquisition will mean to them. The prospective purchaser forgets that the format of the offer may send unintended signals to the parties. Also, such vague offers call into question whether the offeror really understands the process and really has the capabilities to put all the pieces of a reorganization together.

The making of an offer is the time to set the agenda, to build momentum, and to place the parties to the bankruptcy on the defensive. The offeror should be moving into position to control the remainder of the case and to start the process of the rehabilitation of the Chapter 11 company. In other words, taking control of the case at that stage is important to achieving the goals of obtaining the best price and to completing the acquisition process successfully.

The timing of the offer is also very important. If you do not feel that your offer will get the attention it deserves—if, for example, the creditors are unrealistic in their demands—the offer should be put on the shelf for several months while you continue to monitor the case. Conversely, if your offer arrives at a dark hour for the Debtor, it may be quickly adopted by the parties.

Timing is also important in rallying suport to your cause. The Unsecured Creditors' Committee, the bank, and major unsecured creditors should be personally advised of the nature of the offer prior to its official presentation so that they might vocally support it in court from the inception. Once the court permits the solicitation of votes upon the plan, then a program of official and unofficial recommendations by those creditors to the other creditors should be orchestrated.

(This brings us to another conflict between the theories behind the bankruptcy law and the realities. The bankruptcy code states that acceptances to a Plan of Reorganization cannot be solicited until the court enters an order allowing the plan to be sent to the creditors. However, the prudent prospective purchaser will attempt to reach a negotiated agreement with the Unsecured Creditors' Committee and/or the major unsecured creditors on a price that they find satisfactory and will approve before he goes to the trouble of formally presenting a plan proposal. One would think that such an action would be in violation of the law, but it is so important that the judge will put on his blindfold unless someone solicits binding, written voting commitments. Once again, practicality conquers all in the bankruptcy court!)

I recently acted as a business broker for a prospective purchaser of a Chapter 11 company who failed to heed my advice along the aforementioned lines. Instead of moving expeditiously to propose an offer, he waited until management had found an "angel" and moved quickly with an "emergency" motion to sell the company's assets to themselves (see Chapter 12 respecting a "Section 363 sale of assets"). Thus, his offer was formally proposed only a few days before the hearing on management's offer, and there was no time to button up loose ends and pin down details. Also, he did not bother to meet with the Unsecured Creditors' Committee, relying on the fact that he had added a sweetener for the unsecured creditors of additional time payments (with interest) to his cash offer that matched management's proposal. He assumed that the unsecured creditors would recognize the superiority of his offer without a full presentation in person.

As a result the creditors did not realize the prospective purchaser's abilities (he had already turned around a company that made a similar product), or that he was serious about saving the company. As a further result, management was able to portray him (wrongly) as someone interested only in liquidating the assets to acquire pieces of machinery, and to stampede the creditors into sticking with the "devil they knew. ... " Thus, he failed to acquire the company even though he offered the creditors twice as much of a dividend as did management, and I lost a nice broker's fee!

The offer should contain contingencies that protect you during the period until the Plan of Reorganization is confirmed and you can take over the company, some of which are the standard clauses contained in acquisition agreements and some of which are related to the bankruptcy process.

Many items considered important and standard in acquisition agreements are applicable to the Chapter 11 company. The buyer will ordinarily want a clear and precise recitation of the items being purchased, warranties as to their condition, and representations as to their maintenance until the purchase can be closed.

The offer should specify that during the interim period between the making of the offer and the closing, the Chapter 11 company will maintain a certain level of inventories and continue operations only in the ordinary course of business. Perhaps the condition of the Chapter 11 company will call for more specific, stringent limits and requirements. The closing should be contingent on the Debtor maintaining those standards during the interim period, as verified by preclosing inspections. (The preclosing inspections are very important because, as a practical matter, it will be almost impossible to retrieve any portion of the purchase price after it is distributed to creditors.)

The Debtor may be in urgent need of funds to maintain operations that cannot await the closing of the sale; however, the offeror understandably will be reluctant to hand over money prior to being assured of acquiring the company. While it is never a comfortable situation, bankruptcy law allows any such loans to the Debtor to have a *first* lien upon all of the Debtor's property *and* to have what, in bankruptcy parlance, is known as a "superpriority" position ahead of all priority creditors. With that form of security, it is virtually impossible for the prospective purchaser to lose the money advanced to the Debtor, even if the acquisition fails and the Chapter 11 company is liquidated. Thus a "bridge" loan can be used safely to maintain the value of the company during the acquisition process.

The primary bankruptcy-related concern that troubles prospective purchasers is that they do not want to be placed in a position where they have become committed to pay the company's creditors but then are not granted the terms and conditions they have proposed. That concern in unfounded—it is an axiom of bankruptcy practice that the offeror retains total control over his commitment. At the point the prospective purchaser makes his formal offer, it can be essentially on a take-it-or-leave-it basis; if the creditors do not approve the offer, the offeror can simply withdraw from the situation with no financial penalty.

A common protection for the prospective purchaser is that the offer expressly states that it is contingent upon the entry of an order by the bankruptcy judge authorizing the sale of the company. While it is common for the offer to include some "earnest money" deposit, those funds are ordinarily retained in an escrow that provides they shall be returned to the offeror in the event the sale of the assets is not approved. As discussed more fully later, the offer then becomes the catalyst for a party to propose a Plan of Reorganization, which then provides how the funds received from the sale of the company will be applied. When the creditors have voted to approve the plan and the bankruptcy judge has confirmed it, the sale of the company can be closed.

Most offers provide for a closing within a certain number of days after the entry of an order approving a Plan of Reorganization. Therefore, the closing may be delayed because of the time period inherent in acquiring court approval of a plan. If approval seems assured, the period can be used doing those many things and preparing those many documents necessary for the closing, and the bankruptcy process may cause little delay. If the usual sixty-to-ninety-day period for gaining approval is considered too long and if the major creditors are on the purchaser's side, the court usually is quite willing to shorten the time periods, sometimes by more than half.

Now you can see that your offer will set in motion the creation of a Plan of Reorganization. So that you can get a feel for that process, you should have an understanding of how a Plan of Reorganization will be presented to the creditors and to the court for approval, and that will be discussed in the chapter after the next.

Chapter 10

How to Achieve the Lowest Purchase Price

Determining a proper purchase price for a Chapter 11 company is not easy. Standard formulas for valuing a business do not apply to a company in bankruptcy. As has been pointed out, the value of specific assets associated with a troubled company is always open to question. So, how does a purchaser determine the low end of the acceptable price range?

In terms of the gross price, the biggest leeway lies in the amount that will be allocated for the unsecured creditors. With some exceptions that arise when the Chapter 11 company owns valuable real estate or is otherwise asset-rich, the unsecured creditors cannot expect a substantial dividend upon their claims. Of course, you will want to offer as little as possible to the unsecured creditors; however, their votes hold a key to your acquisition of the Chapter 11 company, and it would be an error to offer them a sum that is too small even by the reduced standards of Chapter 11 practice.

Ordinarily several factors will set the lower parameter. First of all, an outrageous low-ball offer that ignores the realities of the case will cause a loss of credibility from which the prospective purchaser may never recover. Secondly, usually a prospective purchaser wants and needs to avoid rejection by the voters of the Plan of Reorganization, since the process of proposing a sweetened amended plan would take an extra month or more.

So how does one determine a safe, substantial, but money-saving amount in cash to offer the unsecured creditors? The answer: *Kallen's Rule-of-Thumb*.

Kallen's Rule-of-Thumb is a semi-scientific formula that takes into account the unsecured creditor's hopes, ambitions, and fears; valuation ranges of the Chapter 11 company's assets; and the best interests of the prospective purchaser. (It does not, however, factor in the owner's horoscope or the phase of the moon on the date of the offer.) Kallen's Rule-of-Thumb may be summarized as follows: offer the unsecured creditors more than they would receive on liquidation of the Debtor, but less than they are happy with. If you fill in the formula with the mathematics of the particular case, you can be confident that the unsecured creditors will, in spite of the howls of pain, acquiesce to your offer.

In some cases, the formula will produce values close to zero. However, as the percentage the unsecured creditors will receive upon their claims nears the zero mark, they are more likely to reject the plan just for the psychological pleasure of it. Accordingly, the prudent purchaser will add a few crumbs to the bare minimum.

If it is irrefutable that the assets are worth no more than the claims of the secured creditors, logically the unsecured creditors should receive nothing whatsoever. However, a caveat comes to mind. Because of the inherent uncertainties in valuing the assets of a Chapter 11 company, the unsecured creditors normally will not concede the issue. As a result, you are facing much contention and what could be an expensive, lengthy hearing concerning valuation of the company. Accordingly, while in some cases it is appropriate to offer the unsecured creditors nothing whatsoever, in borderline cases, it may be worthwhile to offer them a small amount to buy peace and certainty.

Another issue involves the form of the offer to the unsecured creditors. The dividend to unsecured creditors is commonly described as a percentage; that is, the percent of the claim that each unsecured creditor will receive in cash. The Plan of Reorganization may provide that the class of unsecured creditors will receive, say, a five percent dividend. However, that format can present problems for the purchaser as many times the plan must be proposed before all claims have been filed, reviewed, and/or objected to. As a result, a fixed percentage may lead to a total dollar amount that is unacceptably large to the purchaser.

In such circumstances, the prudent course of action is to provide that the class of unsecured creditors will share in a pot funded in a specific amount. For example, the plan may state that the class of unsecured creditors will receive $50,000, to be shared by them *pro rata* based upon the amounts of the claims as they shall later be determined. Besides definitively limiting the amount of the purchaser's commitment, several other goals are served. First, it avoids the delay and acrimony involved in litigating the validity and fixing the amounts of each disputed unsecured claim, by postponing the fights until after the vote on the plan. Second, it leaves the exact percentage ambiguous, and perhaps the unsecured creditors will overestimate their respective dividends. Another result is that it makes the unsecured creditors the real parties in interest to police their brethren's claims, as the process of objecting to claims becomes a "zero-sum game" among the unsecured creditors.

Until now the discussion has centered around cash payments to unsecured creditors upon the approval of the Plan of Reorganization. About now your mind is probably racing ahead to other forms of chiseling the unsecured creditors, including making installment payments and issuing securities. Those methods certainly are available, and will be discussed shortly; however, generally speaking, I recommend that payments to unsecured creditors be made in full upon approval of the plan, or shortly thereafter, if you have the cash.

Payment of the obligation to the unsecured creditors quickly and in cash has several advantages for the purchaser. First, nearly all creditors and creditors' attorneys understand that imputed interest is inherent in delayed payment. That is, receipt of $50,000 a year from now is not equal to receipt of $50,000 today, because that $50,000 received today could be deposited in a bank and could start earning interest, or it could be used to pay down a loan and to avoid the accrual of a certain amount of interest. Consequently, depending on the rate of interest imputed, in order to equal $50,000 paid today, a debtor may have to promise a creditor $55,000 if it is to be paid a year from now. When the *risk* of waiting for that money is factored in, that creditor may want $70,000 in the future. If you can earn that differential on your money in the meantime, it actually will not cost you more to pay "on time," but if you are highly leveraged, all kinds of things can go wrong in the interim.

Another problem is that, if the unsecured creditors are sophisticated or well represented by counsel, they will insist that the bankruptcy court retain jurisdiction over the Chapter 11 company for so long as it owes payments to creditors under the Plan of Reorganization. (Unless such a provision is specifically mandated by court order, the bankruptcy court loses all jurisdiction over the Debtor on confirmation of the plan, and if plan payments are not made, the creditors can only file standard collection suits in state court.) While technically the Debtor is relieved from the usual Chapter 11 court supervision during the payment period, the creditors thus retain easy access to the bankruptcy judge to complain about failures of the company to live up to its bargain, or to otherwise create mischief. On the other hand, quick payment to creditors on approval of the plan rids you of them forever.

Without compromising my preference for a lump-sum payout as opposed to installment payments, I acknowledge that sometimes an installment plan is useful as a gimmick to sweeten the bitter fact that the unsecured creditors will be receiving almost nothing upon their claims. For example, instead of proposing to pay the unsecured creditors nothing at all, they may be offered five percent of their claims over three years which, after figuring for inflation and the cost of money, is less than nothing! The plan proponent may feel that the payments can easily be made from cash flow and that the return to creditors will be too small for them to waste time and attorneys fees making any complaints to the judge if payments are not made exactly on the date due. Of course, such a miniscule dividend can fly only if the creditors understand that they cannot reasonably require a "real" dividend.

If creditors are offered too low a dividend stretched over too long a period of time—or other "funny money," such as offering them a small percentage of future profits—at some point the purchaser loses all credibility and the "know-nothing" faction of the creditors take over. At some point stretched payments or other "cute" payment terms violate Kallen's-Rule-of-Thumb. They simply are not more attractive to the creditors than the liquidation of the company.

There is no prohibition in the bankruptcy code from offering creditors stock or debentures in payment of their claims—"swapping equity for debt"— with or without additional cash payments. In fact, sometimes creditors will press for the issuance of stock to them as a "kicker" or "sweetener" to a cash dividend. The creditors may want to require the company to buy back the stock at a later date, or they may just hope that the stock can be sold later on an open market.

If an installment payment plan makes creditors into former friends who will not go away, making them stockholders is like marrying them! While offering creditors stock is initially the cheapest way to buy into a company, you have in effect made them your partners and they will be second-guessing your every move. The bankruptcy code requires that whatever class of stock is offered to the creditors, it must have voting power and a fair share of power within the corporation.

Future actions cannot be taken without strict adherence to the securities laws. Further, the creditor-stockholders gain the right to know everything about the company's actions and to review the books and records for the asking.

In spite of the foregoing, one type of opportunity, namely the acquisition of a relatively large, public company, may lend itself to a swapping of stock for claims. Because of the size of the numbers, it may be that the creditors claims cannot be paid in cash, even at a reduced percentage. Also, since you may not be able to wipe out the prior stockholders entirely, it will not matter that much to add another class of equity holders. From the creditors' point of view, if the stock is likely to be actively traded in the event of a return to profitability, the chance to improve their bankruptcy dividend by selling on the open market later may have a good deal of appeal.

Another unique aspect of reorganization under Chapter 11 is that the issuance of securities as part of a Plan of Reorganization is *exempt from the securities laws.* The rationale is that the availability of information in bankruptcy, including the disclosures that must be made by the debtor to the creditors at the time the plan is proposed (see the next chapter for a more detailed discussion), makes the securities law disclosure rules unnecessary. Accordingly, as the bankruptcy rules are more vague and less technical than the securities laws, issuing securities as part of a plan can have certain advantages if other factors also indicate the advisability of "going public."

These positive and negative considerations add up to the fact that offering securities to creditors can be a risky business, but it may be advantageous if the new management is prepared to deal with the resulting complexities.

Speaking of public companies, one way to take over a company in Chapter 11 is to buy the claims. The concept is similar to that used by the "corporate raiders" in offering to buy the stock of target companies. If you can acquire enough claims—at a *highly* discounted price, of course—you gain the right to control the destiny of the Chapter 11 company, perhaps even proposing a Plan of Reorganization that makes you majority shareholder in return for cancelling your claims. Even if you do not achieve a takeover, if you have bought the claims cheaply enough and have chosen your target company well, you will make a profit when the Debtor pays you a greater amount through its Plan of Reorganization than you paid to purchase the claims.

Buying claims is not a terribly difficult task, as many creditors are happy to receive even a small sum of cash now for their claims rather than wait out the excruciating Chapter 11 process. Contrary to what you might expect, there is no prohibition in the bankruptcy laws against buying claims, even if done for reasons such as the takeover of a company.

Of course, buying claims is inherently risky because it demands commitment at a time when many issues about the company's future remain unresolved. Still, in the proper situation where the target company is exceedingly desirable, the Debtor is uncooperative, and the creditors are too apathetic to help you, it offers yet another option that exists only through the Chapter 11 process.

While often it is advisable to cash out the unsecured creditors, in most cases it is advantageous to spread out the obligations to certain other creditors. For example, as discussed more fully in the section concerning lining up financing, one goal of the takeover of a Chapter 11 company is to get the company's bank to return to some form of installment loan status. (The same effect can be reached if the buyer receives an installment loan from his bank to "take out" the company's bank.)

Another avenue for spreading out the acquisition cost is to *force* the taxing authorities to accept installment payments, something which cannot be done outside of Chapter 11. Pursuant to the bankruptcy code, priority tax claims may be paid over as long a period as six years from the date of the "assessment" of the tax. While interest must be paid upon the installment payments at statutory rates, piecemeal payment of taxes allows you to obtain an unofficial "loan" from the government to aid your acquisition.

Another strategy is to squeeze the bank.

If the bank's position is poorer than usual, it is possible to make substantial inroads into the principal amount of the bank's claim. However, picking a fight with the bank is recommended only if the value of its collateral is much less than the amount of its claim, and you have other "friends" (such as the Unsecured Creditors' Committee) who will support your acquisition.

If your analysis indicates that the secured claim of the bank is shaky, the banker most likely will have a similar understanding. While initially the banker is unlikely to admit the weakness in his secured position, a program of escalating references to it on your part may lead to a rational discussion of how much the bank's secured claim *really* is. If that comes about, perhaps you can reach a discounted figure for the principal balance when the bank rewrites its note for your takeover.

Why will the bank do this? Because if it does not reach agreement with you and the company is liquidated, it will only receive on its claim the amount the collateral brings at auction. The remainder of its claim will prove worthless. Also, behind your claim negotiating posture lies the threat of *The Cramdown.*

The "cramdown," discussed more fully in Chapter 11, provides a procedure whereby a creditor who objects to its dividend proposed in the Plan of Reorganization can be forced to take it if that creditor is receiving no less than his fair share. If that creditor has voted "no" to the plan, the court will ignore the rejection and the plan will be, in effect, crammed down that creditor's throat. It is a very powerful tool in the hands of the plan proponent.

The philosophical basis of the cramdown when it comes to the secured creditor is that the plan provides a dividend to that creditor that is at least as great as the value of that creditor's collateral. If the creditor objects that the proposed dividend is less than the value of the collateral, the bankruptcy judge holds a valuation hearing. Most bankers shudder at the thought of having a judge determine the value of the collateral and will cut a deal if necessary rather than go to a hearing.

In practice, if the bank's security is of borderline quality or quantity, it may be possible to achieve concessions from the banker without having to actually play the cramdown card. Consequently, whether actually resorted to or merely hinted at, the cramdown offers an avenue to drive down the portion of the acquisition price of a Chapter 11 company that will go to the company's lender.

While it is not illegal for the Plan of Reorganization to provide that the owners shall receive money for their ownership interests, that dividend cannot be paid unless *every single creditor* is paid in full or votes in favor of the plan—two highly unlikely occurrences. Thus the owner's interest is formally erased on the acquisition of the company by an outsider, certainly a far different situation than the purchase of a company outside Chapter 11, yet perfectly consistent with the fact that the creditors of such a company actually have the greatest "investment" in it. Greatly reducing or eliminating the owner's portion of the purchase price is another feature of a Chapter 11 takeover.

The owners may realize belatedly that they are low on the totem pole when it comes to receiving consideration for the sale of the company. However, the cold facts of the case may dictate that they exit with nothing to show for their efforts. Many times the owners are happy to be able to do that, if someone will extricate them from the situation and help them avoid extensive personal liability.

Many times also the owners will exit only kicking and screaming, and you must shift your alliance to the creditors. The creditors can take control of the case from the debtor and cause the keys to the company to be turned over to you.

One way of buying peace is to offer the owners some compensation as executives or consultants during the transition (and perhaps thereafter), and/or for an agreement not to compete with the company in the future. The cash will ease the pain, and the creditors cannot object unless they can prove that the payment is for the ownership interest and not for future services.

The timing of your offer can affect the price greatly.

At the commencement of the case, the Debtors and the creditors are infused with optimism . . . for a while. After the parties have slogged it out in the trenches and things seem to be settling into a stalemate, they become more receptive to alternatives.

If you are confident that you can turn the company around, the best time to make an offer is after the company has suffered setbacks or if the company is continuing on a long downhill slide. If the business starts on an uptick, the owners begin to have visions of funding a plan through improved profits.

Chapter 11

The Logistics of a Chapter 11 Plan of Reorganization

The only legitimate goal of a Chapter 11 case is to secure the approval of a Plan of Reorganization that provides for payment of the company's debt, whether in full or compromised. A number of bankruptcy code sections and bankruptcy rules describe the procedures and requirements for proposing a plan, conducting a vote of the creditors, and securing the approval of a plan's provisions by the bankruptcy judge.

Contrary to popular belief, there is no deadline contained in the code or rules for the filing or approval of a plan. The lack of a statutory deadline is sensible as every case is different, and large or complicated cases may take years to work out even if the parties are diligent. Put another way, once more we see that the balance is subtly tipped in the Debtor's favor and against the liquidation of a Chapter 11 company unless absolutely necessary.

The balance is further tipped in the Debtor's favor by the provision in the code that gives the Debtor the *exclusive* right to propose a Plan of Reorganization within the first 120 days of the filing of the bankruptcy petition, and to achieve approval by the creditors and the judge ("confirmation") within the first 180 days of the case, unless a trustee is appointed. If the Debtor has not proposed a plan within 120 days, it will usually request that the bankruptcy judge extend the exclusive rights to propose and effectuate a plan.

Maintenance of that "exclusive period" is one of the devices that the Debtor uses to keep control of the Chapter 11 case. However, a growing number of bankruptcy judges feel that the balance is tipped too far with respect to the Debtor's control over the plan process. The judges will grant extensions of the "exclusive period" only in especially deserving situations.

Note that the expiration of the "exclusive period" does not act as a deadline for the Debtor to file a Plan of Reorganization; it simply means that any other party in interest, such as a creditor or a shareholder, may file a plan and ask the court to conduct a vote. For example, the creditors' committee may file a plan which calls for the sale of the company to you, and if the creditors and the judge approve, the plan may be effectuated over the protest of the company's owners. If no party chooses to file a plan, the Debtor simply continues to operate under court supervision until someone alters the *status quo*.

Once the "exclusive period" has expired, it is possible that more than one plan may be filed. Although some control and supervision by the court is required to prevent creditor confusion, all plans which meet the basic legal requirements are then presented to the creditors for vote. The creditors may vote to approve more than one plan, in which case the bankruptcy judge must choose one plan to confirm—presumably the one which is better for the creditors.

Some conservative judges enter an order at the commencement of each case, on their own initiative, that sets some arbitrary date as a *deadline* for filing a Plan of Reorganization. As a result the Debtor is required to file a quick plan, beg the court for an extension, or risk an order of liquidation. Whether a judge is bluffing or whether he will blindly refuse a request for extension and order conversion to a Chapter 7 liquidation case is always a matter of conjecture, and so the creditors gain some leverage as the deadline nears.

While neither the bankruptcy code nor the bankruptcy rules specify how much a Debtor must pay its creditors, they do contain certain requirements concerning the form and content of the Plan of Reorganization. The plan must:

1. classify claims and interests (e.g., secured, unsecured, etc.);
2. specify how each class will be treated (e.g., debt compromised, payment stretched out, debt paid per its terms, etc.);
3. describe the means for achieving the payment promised in the plan (e.g., from investor, from sale of company, etc.); and
4. allow creditors receiving stock to have voting rights and a fair share of power within the reorganized corporation.

A plan cannot be confirmed unless the liabilities are divided into appropriate classes. As stated in Chapter 7, the simplest and most common divisions are: priority creditors; secured creditors; unsecured creditors, and stockholders. A class cannot contain dissimilar types of claims or interests—e.g., mixing secured and unsecured creditors. Certain priority claims must stand alone, by statute. Also, because each secured claim is usually unique in its terms and treatment of collateral, ordinarily each such claim forms its own class.

A group of similar claims can be divided into multiple classes. The Debtor may wish to isolate one subgroup that will probably reject the plan or that will require a higher payment than the other subgroup(s). For example, the plan may separately classify bank unsecured creditors and trade unsecured creditors, or may place personal injury claimants in their own class. If one subgroup rejects the plan, at least the other may approve it, and the rejecting class may be subjected to a "cramdown." The problem with such fine tuning of classes is that frequently the class receiving poorer treatment fails to see the legitimacy of the division and contests the class distinction and/or works to sabotage approval of the plan.

After the plan describes the nature of the claims contained in each class, it must then state what will be done with each class. Claims within a class must be treated equally.

The plan also must state how the Debtor will acquire the wherewithal to make the payments to the creditors under the plan, and the projection must have some reasonable basis in reality. For example, a plan of a company unprofitable in the recent past that proposes to pay one million dollars to creditors out of the next two year's profits may be considered unrealistic, absent some very favorable, demonstrable change in the business's situation. Such a plan may be found to be "not feasible," and therefore not confirmable, by the bankruptcy judge even if the creditors have voted approval.

The only outright plan prohibition in the bankruptcy code is that in a Chapter 11 filed by an individual person, his or her "exempt" property cannot be sold, leased, or used without the consent of that Debtor.

Thus we have a very large category of permissive provisions for a Plan of Reorganization. The plan may provide for the rejection of executory contracts, the sale of all or part of the Debtor's assets (even including the liquidation of the Debtor), or the continued supervision by the court of installment payments to creditors. Basically, the content of a plan is limited only by the ingenuity and relative bargaining power of the parties in interest. (A relatively straightforward sample Plan of Reorganization is included as Appendix E.)

When the bankruptcy laws were rewritten, the drafters wished to improve the quality of creditor involvement in the reorganization process. If, they reasoned, the key to a democracy is an informed electorate, the bankruptcy law should require disclosure to the creditors of important and relevant facts about the Debtor before they are called upon to vote on a Plan of Reorganization. Thus was born the "Disclosure Statement."

Before a Plan of Reorganization can be disseminated to creditors, the plan proponent must produce a Disclosure Statement and have it approved by the bankruptcy judge in a hearing held with at least twenty-five days prior notice to creditors. (Here the concept gets slightly schizophrenic. All creditors get written notice of the hearing from the bankruptcy court clerk by mail so that they might express their views if they find the disclosure is inadequate. However, because the Disclosure Statement has not yet been approved, it is not sent to the creditors for their review! The result is that the major active parties to the case—the Debtor, the creditors' committee, the bank, and the U.S. Trustee—who receive copies of the Disclosure Statement directly from the plan proponent, dominate the hearing.) Once the Disclosure Statement is approved, the plan and Disclosure Statement may then be sent together to the body of creditors, who then vote to accept or reject the plan.

The bankruptcy code does not list the required contents of a Disclosure Statement; rather, it provides that it must contain adequate information to enable a reasonable creditor to make an informed judgment about the merits of the plan, in light of the nature of the Debtor and the state of its books and records. In order to adequately inform creditors, the Disclosure Statement should provide some history of the company and place its troubles in context, discuss what it has done to improve its situation, and advise as to what it intends to accomplish in the future. The statement also should describe and analyze the Debtor's assets and liabilities. Special circumstances, such as lawsuits, should be disclosed. Of course, creditors should be advised of how the Debtor will manage to pay them the amounts promised in the plan. The contents of Disclosure Statements can vary so widely, it's impossible to include a "typical" one in the appendix.

The plan proponent's statements respecting projections and valuations are supposed to be based on some factual basis, but verification by an independent source is not required. The Debtor will often provide sufficiently dire liquidation values of its assets to remind creditors of how badly they will get burned if they reject the plan and the case is converted to a Chapter 7 liquidation. Values of assets and projections of profits can be quite subjective, sometimes to the point of being downright wishful. In other words, the Debtor can usually get away with a good deal of b.s. as long as it does not cross over into making obvious, blatant lies.

As a result, while sometimes the bankruptcy disclosure process is likened to that mandated by the federal securities laws, in actuality the Disclosure Statement is not held up to the standards of a prospectus. As a practical matter, the Disclosure Statement is more like an advertisement, attempting to educate and to sell the product while not overstepping the boundaries of "puffing."

Once the bankruptcy judge approves the Disclosure Statement, it may be sent to creditors, stockholders, and other parties in interest along with the Plan of Reorganization, a "Ballot for Accepting or Rejecting Plan" on an official form (see Appendix F), and a notice advising when and where ballots must be filed and the date, time, and place of the hearing at which the bankruptcy judge will consider whether to confirm the plan. Remember that the plan must receive approval not only by the creditors but also by the bankruptcy judge, as more fully discussed in the section on confirmation contained later in this chapter.

Approval by the creditors simply consists of achieving the requisite votes in favor of the plan, by class. A class of creditors will be deemed to have approved the plan if a majority in number *and* at least two-thirds in amount of claims *of those voting* cast their votes for acceptance. The dual requirement gives both large and small creditors a voice in the reorganization. Note that a failure to vote is an abstention, not a "no" vote as it was under bankruptcy law prior to the enactment of the bankruptcy code—another Pro-Debtor change, but certainly defensible as simply being in line with our general concept of the democratic process. Thus those that do not vote have their fate decided by those that do.

The amount of each creditor's claim is determined by the filed claim, or, if no claim has been filed, by the amount listed in the schedules. If there is a dispute, the court may be asked to determine provisionally the amount for purposes of the vote. If the Debtor seriously wishes to challenge either the amount or the existence of a claim, it should file a formal objection to that claim and have the bankruptcy judge hold a hearing before the plan is considered.

Shareholders and debentureholders whose interests are negatively affected by the plan each form a class and are entitled to vote. Since each unit is equal within the class, approval of either such class requires an affirmative vote of two-thirds of the units for which votes are cast.

Only those classes whose interests are "impaired" may vote—unimpaired classes are conclusively deemed to have accepted the plan. For example, a class whose claims are to be paid in full in cash, or a secured creditor to whom the collateral is turned over, need not vote. While the "impairment" concept seems straightforward, it can lead to curve balls.

The bankruptcy code provides that a secured creditor is not impaired if the Debtor cures all defaults and promises to adhere to the original security agreement in the future, even over the objections of that creditor. On occasion the plan will propose a form of payment to a secured creditor the plan proponents say is the "same thing" that the creditor was entitled to, while the creditor says that it is not. If the plan proponent can persuade the judge that its convoluted proposal amounts to a complete cure of the prior defaults and puts the secured creditor in the same place it would have been—a place that the secured creditor often contests—the secured creditor is conclusively deemed to have accepted the plan, and the Debtor can avoid the risk that the secured creditor will vote to reject the plan.

Another common tactic, of benefit both to the Debtor and the creditors, is to create a class of small unsecured claims and pay those creditors in full. The bankruptcy code expressly allows such a treatment, for the administrative convenience of not having to pay very small amounts. The real reason most plan proponents do it is to avoid the almost certain "no" vote, for example, of the five-hundred-dollar creditor who will receive twenty-five dollars under a five percent plan. A common plan provision is to pay any unsecured creditor in full whose claim is three hundred dollars or less or who chooses to reduce its claim to three hundred dollars, thus, for example, effectively bringing all claims up to six thousand dollars into the umimpaired, nonvoting class with respect to a five percent plan.

It is not uncommon for a plan to declare a class or classes low on the hierarchy of interests to be totally wiped out. The grounds are that each such class would receive nothing upon a liquidation (due to the strict rules that each higher class would have to be paid in full first) and so it does not deserve to receive anything upon a reorganization. Sometimes it is said that each such wiped-out class does not get a vote because it is "unimpaired;" that is, because the value of its claims or other interests was really zero anyway. It is more accurate to say that each such class is "impaired" (to the max!) and that it need not vote because it is deemed to have rejected the plan, but that the plan nevertheless may be approved pursuant to cramdown provisions, discussed below.

The presiding bankruptcy judge must hold a hearing, on twenty-five-day notice to all interested parties, to "confirm" that the plan has received the requisite number of votes for acceptance and that it otherwise conforms to the legal requirements for final approval by the court.

Counting the vote is usually very straightforward, although occasionally a vote is challenged as procured by fraud or in violation of the solicitation rules or as having arrived too late, etc. If *every* impaired class has voted to accept the plan, the plan has achieved the requisite creditor approval. (The court will have previously ruled on the issue of which classes are unimpaired.)

About now you are probably thinking that the process is very harsh if the plan proponent can come this far and yet be defeated by the failure of any one class to accept the plan, especially since ordinarily each secured creditor forms its own class. Does one dissenting class constitute an unchallengeable veto? What is a plan proponent to do?

The answer is that at the confirmation hearing, the plan proponent requests the bankruptcy judge to "cram down" the plan on each rejecting class. That is, the judge is asked to declare that, pursuant to specific considerations discussed below, the *dissenting class is being treated fairly and so its rejection of the plan is illegitimate,* and it will be deemed to have accepted the plan. (Democracy has its limits, even—or especially—in bankruptcy court. The plan is thus virtually crammed down the throats of the parties in the rejecting class!) Per the bankruptcy code, if at least *one* class of impaired creditors votes to accept the plan, every other class is subject to cramdown.

The cramdown—what a wonderful, descriptive term—may be applied against a class by the judge if he finds that:

1. the class is not being discriminated against "unfairly"—that is, no creditors with similar types of claims have been put in a separate class and given better treatment; and
2. the treatment of the class is "fair and equitable"—a bankruptcy

term-of-art which means that no class lower in the hierarchy receives anything unless and until the crammed-down class receives one hundred percent of its claims.

The method of cramming down a class varies depending on the type of class.

If the Debtor wishes to cram down a secured creditor—that is, have the plan confirmed by the judge in spite of the rejection by that class-of-one—the plan must offer to pay that creditor the full value of its *secured* claim, in one of several ways. The plan may provide that all of that creditor's collateral will be turned over to it; that the collateral will be sold and the secured creditor will receive all the proceeds; or that the Debtor will pay for the present value of the collateral either in cash or upon payments which provide interest. The Debtor may even substitute collateral as long as it is equivalent to the original.

What is the advantage to the Debtor, if it must recognize the full value of the secured creditor's collateral? First of all, it removes veto power from a creditor that has unreasonably voted "no." Second, it allows the secured portion of the claim to be limited to the present value of the collateral *as valued by the judge,* a process most secured creditors fear. (The portion of the claim that exceeds the value of the collateral becomes an unsecured claim.) Third, it shifts the Debtor's payment obligation away from the strict terms of the security agreement and allows the Debtor, with court approval, to force the secured creditor to accept the Debtor's payment schedule. The Debtor may even propose a different interest rate. The court then determines if it is an appropriate "market" interest rate, an issue that provokes much dispute.

In extreme cases, the Debtor may offer something that looks nothing like the original arrangement, as long as it can persuade the court that the proposal provides for an "equivalent" obligation. For example, the plan may offer an equipment financier payment in bonds secured by accounts receivable. In other words, the deal is rewritten by the Debtor and the bankruptcy judge over the creditor's objection (as in "cram down").

The secured creditor is left a little wiggle room. It may exercise a right provided by the bankruptcy code to have its entire *claim* treated as secured even though the value of the collateral may be less than the amount of the claim. However, if the secured creditor elects to do that, the payments to that creditor need only total the principal amount of the claim, and that creditor is not paid interest or any other compensation for delayed payment.

You may have questions about the cramdown that have not been answered here, but I do not apologize. The secured creditor cramdown is quite a complicated stunt and is not for amateurs to attempt without the guidance of experienced bankruptcy counsel. Please remember that this book is designed to provide the prospective investor or purchaser with a business person's overview of the process and is not a legal treatise on bankruptcy. It will have served its purpose if such technical discussions give you some idea of the *flexibility* of the bankruptcy process, which can be used by the Debtor, purchaser, or investor.

While the bankruptcy code also allows for the cramdown of unsecured creditors, the requirements are so unpalatable to the Debtor that it is seldom done. To effectuate a plan over the rejection of a class of unsecured creditors, that class must be paid the total amount of its claims—out of the question, in most cases—or all lower classes of interests must be totally wiped out. Since one of those lower classes consists of the owner's interest, an unsecured creditor cramdown is not a very interesting proposition for the people who control the Debtor. To paraphrase a wartime saying, no owner wants to say "I had to destroy my interest in the company in order to save it."

The practical result is that plan proponents do not attempt to cram down unsecured creditors. They offer them a few pennies and remind them that if they reject the plan and the company is liquidated, they will almost certainly receive nothing at all. In fact, rarely do unsecured creditors reject a plan if the Debtor knowingly or unknowingly follows Kallen's Rule-Of-Thumb for dealing with unsecured creditors: offer them more than they would receive on liquidation but less than makes them happy!

While most plans leave the equity holders with their ownership interests intact—thus leaving them unimpaired and conclusively in acceptance of the plan—classes of equity holders may also be subject to cramdown. As with unsecured creditors, they must be paid the face value of their interests; if paid less, then every class lower in priority (that is, subordinated equity interests) must be wiped out.

Once the vote has been counted—or ignored, in the case of the cramdown—and the bankruptcy judge has determined that the Plan of Reorganization has the requisite creditor acceptance, the judge must then confirm that the plan meets certain legal standards before it can have final court approval.

In order to confirm a Plan of Reorganization, the court must make findings to the effect that:

1. the plan was proposed in good faith;
2. the plan proponents did not use illegal means to gain creditor acceptance;
3. the plan does not contain any provisions prohibited by, or fail to include terms required by, the bankruptcy code;
4. the plan provisions must be in the "best interests" of the creditors and equity security holders (read: they will be no worse off under the plan than they would be if the case were converted to that under Chapter 7 and the Debtor liquidated);
5. each priority claim will be paid either (a) in full, (b)pursuant to a payment plan specifically authorized by the bankruptcy code for certain categories of debts, or (c) in lesser amount *only if that creditor consents;*
6. the plan proposals are "feasible," that is, the Debtor will be able to make the promised payments, and it is not likely that the Debtor's performance of the obligations contained in the plan will lead to liquidation or another reorganization of the Debtor; and
7. the *principal* purpose of the plan, if it has been objected to by the government, is not to avoid taxes or the securities laws.

The "good faith" requirement is in the law to allow a bankruptcy judge to deny confirmation on his own initiative, in spite of creditor consent, where it appears that the results of the reorganization will not be consistent with recognized goals of the bankruptcy laws. For example, confirmation may be denied where a fraud is being perpetrated on creditors.

There are two principal reasons why the bankruptcy code limits democracy by providing the judge with these veto powers. The first is that, as the "election judge," he should not stand by while creditors are defrauded by illegal acts of the plan proponents. The second is that, by requiring court supervision over the plan provisions and procedures, the bankruptcy code provides the moral basis for taking economic rights away from dissenters.

In the case where the owners are uncooperative to a reorganization proposal and the Debtor's "exclusive period" has ended, any creditor may propose a Plan of Reorganization. Accordingly, the prospective purchaser may become aligned with the creditors in the plan approval process.

The procedures mandated in the bankruptcy code and rules for acquiring confirmation of a Plan of Reorganization are no different for the plan proposed by a creditor than for that promulgated by the Debtor. The law is blind to the identity of the plan proponent and to the fact that the creditor's plan will result in a takeover of the Chapter 11 company that is unwanted by its owners. However, there are a few practical differences that arise when the owners have not proposed the plan, none of which make the process more onerous.

One difference which is actually a great help to the purchaser is that creditor sponsorship should virtually guarantee that the creditor body will vote to approve the plan. Presumably the sponsoring creditor will have enough incentive and clout to persuade the other creditors of its benefits. If the plan is sponsored by the Unsecured Creditors' Committee, the process is a cakewalk. Including the bank and/or influential unsecured creditors as sponsors of the plan is always helpful.

Preparation of the Disclosure Statement presents a problem, as the sponsoring creditor(s) will not wish to certify the accuracy of financial information about the Debtor that is usually placed in it. On the other hand, it is generally considered inappropriate for a creditors' plan to ignore the Disclosure Statement requirement altogether. In most cases a practical compromise is effectuated, whereby the plan proponents prepare and circulate a Disclosure Statement (with court approval) that includes financial information previously provided to the creditors or contained in reports filed with the court. The statement contains a disclaimer by which the plan proponents advise the creditors that they do not—and because of circumstances, cannot—warrant the accuracy of the information contained in it.

The end result is a failure for the philosophy behind the disclosure requirements, but a triumph (as usual) for the practical side of bankruptcy court practice. The judges recognize the benefits to the creditors of allowing them to proceed with their plan, and the securities-law model of disclosure is forgotten. As a result, consideration by the creditor body and the court is founded upon what may be incomplete or inaccurate information. However, there do not seem to be any alternatives if the law is going to provide for the effectuation of Plans of Reorganization proposed by creditors.

As with a proposal sponsored by the Debtor, your offer sponsored by the creditors may contain specific limitations on its term, requirement as to maintenance of the status quo as to the Debtor's operations during the plan approval process, and contingencies that must be accomplished before a closing can take place. If there is some fear that the owners of the Chapter 11 company will damage the business in the interim period, the creditors can improve substantially upon their supervision of the Debtor. They may also acquire orders from the bankruptcy judge that expressly and specifically limit the Debtor's actions pending the confirmation of the plan.

If a substantial amount of claims is purchased at a heavily discounted price, the prospective purchaser of the company may then propose the Plan of Reorganization as a creditor. By buying a claim, the outsider gains all of the rights of a creditor, and there is no prohibition under the law from a creditor furthering its own interests by acquiring the Debtor. The aforementioned acquisition is the bankruptcy equivalent of the totally unwanted takeover because it assumes that the purchaser does not have the support of either the Debtor's owner or the influential creditors, and that the takeover will be accomplished by persuading "the masses" of the creditors to vote approval. You can see that such a procedure is a hard way to go, but it certainly is a viable option in the situation where the major creditors are not hostile to you but rather are simply too apathetic to actively propose and support a Plan of Reorganization.

The process of proposing a Plan of Reorganization also sets other bankruptcy procedures in motion. A deadline date for the filing of claims must be set and the body of creditors fixed for the purpose of voting on the plan.

The process of establishing the claims provides for two options. Ordinarily the claims are accepted at face value for the purpose of voting, the plan proponent reserving the right to challenge the validity and amount of claims after the confirmation hearing. However, sometimes the plan proponent may wish to neutralize a troublesome creditor with a questionable claim, and by objecting to the claim before the plan is considered that creditor's vote may be cancelled or diminished in effect. Aside from voting considerations, if the plan provides for a lump sum to be shared by the unsecured creditors, the plan proponent has no real interest in any objections to claims and those matters will be left to other parties in interest. Consequently, the format of the plan and the facts of the case will dictate if and when you object to creditors' claims.

Bankruptcy law provides that the Plan of Reorganization should state which "executory" contracts and leases will be reaffirmed by the Debtor and which will be rejected. (Remember that in the case of rejection, the other party to the contract or lease becomes a general unsecured creditor and receives compensation only in the same proportion of the claim as do the preexisting unsecured creditors.)

In the situation where the plan is funded by the sale of the Debtor's assets to a new entity, the Debtor should affirm desirable contracts and leases and then assign them to the new entity. However, there is a note of caution: while the bankruptcy law forces outside parties to accept the Debtor as a party to the contract or lease if the Debtor brings its obligations up to date, it does not cover the following assignment to another entity. Assignment rules are covered by the terms of the contract or lease and state law. Accordingly, the purchaser of the business should take care to mend fences with a company for which retention of the relationship, and the underlying contract or lease, is very important to the acquired business.

Another item of importance, discussed more fully earlier in this book, may be the claims of the Debtor under the bankruptcy "preference" or "fraudulent conveyance" laws to return to the Debtor assets which previously had been transferred, or payments to creditors which previously had been made, by the Debtor. If those claims have been left to the creditors as a sweetener, the purchaser will have no interest in them. However, if those rights have been retained, in some cases they can result in significant funds being returned to the company.

Once the Plan of Reorganization has been confirmed and the company is outside direct court and creditor supervision, it is supposed to follow the mandates of the plan religiously. In practice the creditors are not too quick to complain to the bankruptcy court if the former Debtor is remiss (if they have retained that right), and so the new company has some practical leeway in performing its obligations under the plan. In cases where conforming to the payment schedule contained in the plan is proving impossible, the company may ask the court to reopen the case for the purpose of allowing it to file a modified Plan of Reorganization and seek approval of the amended proposal. Surprisingly, there is no prohibition against the company filing another Chapter 11. If at first you do not succeed....

Chapter 12

Variations on the Theme

A basic assumption of this text is that the reader desires to obtain the ownership and control of a Chapter 11 company for the purposes of establishing himself as the chief operating officer. Another assumption is that the reader wishes to exercise that level of control solely or along with a partner who joins with him in the acquisition of the company. However, the concepts and strategies presented here apply equally well for the person who merely would like to be an "investor," that is, a person who infuses capital into a company and in return becomes a stockholder but not an active participant in the day-to-day management of the company.

Becoming an investor may completely fulfill the objectives of a person who wants a more "personal" business investment but who cannot or will not serve as a full-time employee. The benefits accrue as the labor and talent of the executives of the company provide profits for the investor. If the investor chooses wisely, the psychological and financial rewards from participating in a turnaround can far exceed those available on the stock markets.

The *sine qua non* of the Chapter 11 investment is the determination by the investor that the target company has strong, competent, honest management capable of orchestrating a turnaround if provided with sufficient financing. It requires a recognition that Chapter 11 status is not always the result of managerial incompetence. It must separate an isolated error by management from chronic failures of judgment or will.

The advantages of investing in a Chapter 11 company are twofold. First, of course, is the tremendous "bang for the buck" the investment can achieve in wiping out debts and producing a solid balance sheet. Second, the investor's leverage over the owners of the company at the time of the investment is far greater in the Chapter 11 situation, allowing far greater returns, perks, safeguards, percentage of ownership, etc., than in the usual nonbankruptcy investment.

The tax situation of the Debtor may provide great benefits to an investor. As discussed more fully earlier, if the investor acquires less than fifty percent of the common stock and the nature of the company's business remains the same, he may enjoy the benefits of future profits sheltered by past "net operating losses."

A hybrid situation may occur when a prospective purchaser discovers that it would be advantageous to retain the owners of the Chapter 11 company in the reorganized business. Since the new owner and the old owners will have to share control, the "chemistry" must be just right. However, the management that combines past experience in the business with fresh ideas and money can be quite strong indeed.

Flexibility to exit the situation can be built into the investment by providing for "puts" (when the investor can require the company to buy him out) or "calls" (when the company can require the investor to sell his stock to the company). Thus should the "chemistry" produce a volatile mixture, the parties can disassociate.

The principles for taking a company out of Chapter 11 are no different when there is an investment in, rather than a purchase of, the company. As with the purchaser, the investor provides the funding necessary for the company to propose a Plan of Reorganization. Upon approval of the plan, the company emerges from Chapter 11. The only difference is that in the case of an investment in the company, the ownership of the reorganized company is shared between the owner who initiated the Chapter 11 and the "angel" who stepped in to help save the company.

You could become a lender.

This book is not written for institutional lenders—if it were, writing it would have been a waste of time. Chapter 11 companies present the antithesis of circumstances mandated by bankers' views of "Sound Lending Practices." Almost never will a bank or finance company provide turnaround financing. Almost never are the Chapter 11 company's circumstances such that an infusion of funds will produce a dramatic and guaranteed increase in collateral and profitability—and that is what the institutional lenders require in such a situation. In other words, bankers do not keep their jobs by being heroes.

In fact, a major reason why I wrote this book was to help deserving

Chapter 11 companies find funding in a situation where knocking on the doors to the banks will only produce frustration.

There is no law that says an individual or a group of individuals cannot lend money to a troubled company. Sometimes making a loan may be advantageous for the financier, largely because of the *very* attractive interest rate that is likely to be in the offing. Since the loan proceeds will be used to pay off a substantial amount of debts, the balance sheet after the plan is confirmed may justify a loan and may provide reasonable amount of security.

The problem is that the loan made in such a circumstance is inherently more risky than made to a company with a history of profits. The loan is, in essence, venture capital, and funds provided in such a situation usually bestow an ownership interest and a degree of control to the "angel" which a loan does not provide.

Where there is a will, there is a way. The loan can be made under terms that provide "trip wires" and standards for the debtor's operations. The lender may be granted a seat on the board of directors. The lack of an ownership interest may be more than compensated for by the generous interest terms. Thus safeguards can be instituted, while the commitment of the financier, and the term of his involvement, remain strictly limited.

A reasonable amount of security can usually be provided. If a portion of the loan is used to "take out" the bank, the private lender can acquire a first lien on all of the assets. If the bank is not fully repaid, perhaps a compromise can be reached, capping the amount of the bank's first lien or splitting the assets in which each lender will have a first lien. Normally a bank does not like to enter into such a compromise, but it will do so if it feels that the additional loan will improve the Debtor's business and thereby improve the quality of its loan. Of course, the quality of the private lender's collateral will not be of a level required by an institutional lender, but it may be sufficient to satisfy an individual with an entrepreneurial bent—who is receiving a fat interest rate.

While it is a rather high stakes game, the loan may be used as a method of taking over a company. It may be that the lender has a strong feeling that the Debtor will not be able to fulfill its obligations and will become subject to foreclosure. The lender may be ready and willing to oust the owners and take sole control over operations. The unpaid portion of the loan then becomes the "price" of acquiring the company, and it may be much less than would be required for a straightforward purchase. The more common situation is that the lender hopes that the loan will be repaid, but stands ready to take over the borrower if necessary.

It is not uncommon for a financier to negotiate a hybrid situation, where his funding buys him a certain amount of stock and a portion of the funds are designated as a loan to be repaid upon specific terms. If he can negotiate a deal whereby a small amount of capital contribution leads to the acquisition of a large percentage of a company's stock, and the major portion of his funding is deemed to be a loan, the financier has managed to achieve the best of both worlds. If all goes well, most of his funding will be repaid to him, with interest, and he will remain as a substantial, if not a majority, shareholder.

Such a result shows the great bargaining power that the financier possessed under the circumstances. (The ultimate situation involves a total buyout where the purchaser designates nearly all of the purchase price as a loan to the company, since there is no one except the Internal Revenue Service to tell him how much must be designated as capital.)

Another option along the investment-loan continuum is to use the loan format as a form of hedging an investment in the company. At the initial stage, the funding is deemed to be wholly or mostly a loan, and the former owner remains as the entire, or the majority, owner. However, the underlying agreement may provide that at later stages, upon the discretion of the financier, all or portions of the loan may be converted to a capital contribution and stock issued. Thus the financier retains the right to juggle the balance between his loan and capital commitments.

To review, the standard procedure for reorganizing a company in Chapter 11 is to propose a Plan of Reorganization that is then voted upon by the creditors and confirmed by the court. The legal entity that filed the case, usually a corporation, then emerges from bankruptcy. The bankruptcy code and rules devote a fair amount of text to the procedures involving the plan; it is the legally favored means of saving a troubled company.

However, one terse subsection of the bankruptcy code [§363(b)(1)] provides an alternative to the Plan of Reorganization by providing that the Chapter 11 company may sell assets outside the ordinary course of business upon prior approval of the bankruptcy judge. Consequently, the company may sell all, or substantially all, of its assets, go out of business, and let the creditors divide the proceeds according to the hierarchy set by the bankruptcy code. It is not even necessary that the assets be sold to an already existing entity. A new corporation may be formed to accept the assets.

Section 363 offers many advantages to the investor or purchaser. First, it can be effectuated much quicker than a Plan of Reorganization. Following the code-mandated procedures for plan confirmation takes sixty days at best, and most likely more, due to notice requirements for the required hearings on the disclosure statement and, then, the plan confirmation. If the judge wants changes in the disclosure statement or plan, additional hearings may be required. On the other hand, assets may be sold upon motion made to the court, with twenty days notice to creditors.

A second advantage of the sale of assets is that it only requires the approval of the judge. No creditor vote. No confirmation standards. Simply persuade the judge that it is a good idea and it is a "done deal." Of course, creditors may appear at the hearing and make their objections known, but they have no veto or voting power.

Another element of the bankruptcy law that should give a buyer of the assets of a Chapter 11 company comfort has to do with a creditor's ability to challenge the sale. Outside bankruptcy, most state laws require that the sale of a substantial portion of a company's assets (a "bulk sale") be done only upon notice to creditors, giving them time to respond in many ways including the filing of a lawsuit. If such an action is taken, the deal is virtually dead because the outcome of the challenge cannot be determined until after a long period of litigation. However, bankruptcy law provides only a very limited chance to block a §363 sale.

If a creditor objects to a §363 sale, it must oppose it in a court hearing. If the objector prevails, there is no sale and the purchaser simply walks away from the deal—somewhat bewildered, no doubt, but financially whole. If the court denies the objection and orders the sale, the creditor can block the sale *only if it files an appeal with a bond in excess of the amount of the sale price, before the sale is closed,* and requests that the sale be "stayed" by the court. I have yet to see an objector brave enough and sure enough of its position to put that much on the line for an appeal of a sale. (Why is the limitation on appeals so Draconian? To *encourage* outsiders to buy assets out of bankruptcy.)

Consequently, unlike the rather ambiguous effects of an acquisition made outside of court, possible objections and contingent liabilities are clearly and quickly cut off. The only loss will be that any state and local transfer taxes must be paid, while transfers pursuant to a Plan of Reorganization are exempt.

Obviously there is great incentive to avoid the complicated and time-consuming plan process, especially when there is an outside buyer and he wants to take over *now*. So why is the Plan of Reorganization format used ninety percent of the time? Because it is *supposed* to be, say the judges.

While the bankruptcy code and rules are silent as to when the sale of assets may be used as the reorganization format, the courts have recognized that the plan process, with its safeguards, is the preferred method. The appellate court decisions say that the Debtor should have to prove some great emergency to reorganize through a sale of assets, such as a threatened rapid diminution in the value of those assets, lack of capital to operate the company, etc. Accordingly, the bankruptcy judges are loathe to permit the Debtor to take the fast track unless there is some compelling reason. However, I have seen judges so anxious to please the debtor and so unmindful of the goal of creditor participation that quick approval of a §363 sale of assets becomes the ultimate cramdown, even in nonemergency situations.

Thus, while a §363 sale of assets may not be appropriate in every situation, the prospective purchaser should keep it in mind when making an offer for a Chapter 11 company and should consult with bankruptcy counsel respecting its usefulness under the circumstances of the case.

What about putting a company into Chapter 11? It is not a question of being nasty and spiteful. We are talking about using the bankruptcy process with the cooperation of the target company's owners.

Let us assume that you have located a troubled company that is not in Chapter 11, and you believe that you have the basis of a deal to acquire it. However, you are worried about potential claims lurking off the books, and you do not feel that the company can be successful with its present debt load. Buying such a company outside of Chapter 11 can be messy and risky. Your best option may be to run the company through Chapter 11 before you acquire it.

Instead of a normal acquisition offer, you advise the owners that you will not purchase the company outside of a Chapter 11 case, but that you will make a firm offer to fund a Chapter 11 Plan of Reorganization as part of your acquisition. The owners may have no choice but to accede if they otherwise cannot "unload" their troubled company.

The logistics consist of *filing the Plan of Reorganization at the same time as the Chapter 11 case is filed.* There is no law against it. The creditors will not know what hit them. All claims must be funnelled through the bankruptcy process. Control of the case remains firmly in the Debtor's hands. Within three months you will be the owner of a reorganized company. The procedure would have been greatly appreciated by Niccolo Machiavelli, who counseled in *The Prince* (published in 1513) that when a person in power finds that he must do distasteful acts, he should do them quickly (and ruthlessly) and thus put them behind him before others can react.

Chapter 13

Emerging From Bankruptcy (Or, You Have Done It! Now What?)

Disengaging from bankruptcy court is so easy that it is almost anticlimactic.

Once the bankruptcy judge has entered the order confirming the Plan of Reorganization, supervision over the Chapter 11 company's activities ceases. If there is no litigation pending, the judge has no reason to have additional hearings. The United States Trustee requires no further reports. The clerk of the bankruptcy court will soon close the court file and pack it off to storage. For the former Debtor, the silence is almost eerie.

Some litigation may outlive the reorganization. The court may be hearing objections to claims and preference and fraudulent conveyance complaints. However, if those matters have been left for the benefit of the creditors, the former Debtor may have only a tangential role. If you have chosen to remain involved in the litigation for the benefit of the "new" company, that involvement does not in any way increase court supervision over the business operations going forward.

The main continuing effect of the bankruptcy upon the former Debtor will be the duties imposed by the Plan of Reorganization. If installment payments to creditors are to be made, ordinarily they are to be self-executing; the former debtor is expected to send the proper checks to the creditors when payments come due. Some bankruptcy judges schedule a "status call" at the conclusion of the payment schedule just to require the former Debtor to confirm to the court that the payments have been made. However, many judges do not have even that minimal a program and will not concern themselves with compliance unless a creditor complains. Unless the creditors have acquired a clause in the confirmation order retaining the right to complain about breaches of the plan payments, the bankruptcy judge loses jurisdiction and cannot hear those complaints at all.

A benefit of buying a company out of Chapter 11 is that, with certain unlikely and theoretical exceptions (and with the possible exception of environmental liability, the limits of which have not yet been fully litigated), the purchaser can be assured that the "new" company will not be subject to any liabilities that plagued the Chapter 11 company. The standard contractual terms offer a pretty good buffer, and a number of elemental aspects of the bankruptcy process combine to add protections not otherwise available. For example, all claimants against the Debtor are required to prosecute their claims *only* through bankruptcy court and can *only* look to the Debtor's bankruptcy estate for payment. In other words, the consideration the purchaser provides to the creditors through the Plan of Reorganization is the only dividend those creditors can collect from the Chapter 11 company or its successors.

While I cannot guarantee a one hundred percent barrier as case law continues to develop, the bankruptcy process until now has proven very effective at cutting off claims against the new company based on "successor liability" for acts of the old company. While that type of claim is growing for acquisitions outside of bankruptcy, for acquisitions through the bankruptcy process additional substantial hurdles exist for the claimant.

Thus the creditors are forever barred from pursuing their claims against the former Debtor, its successors, and/or the purchaser of the former Debtor's assets except insofar as provided for in the Plan of Reorganization. To do so is to act in "contempt of court," and the former Debtor always has the right to return to bankruptcy court to ask for sanctions against any creditor that does not heed the dictates of the bankruptcy laws.

It is important that you "hold the line" when those creditors call you to beg, plead, and threaten in a final effort to improve their percentage of payment. You might tell them that you would love to pay them, but the bankruptcy law and your lawyer will not allow it. Also, you might remind them that it was not you who ran up the debts, it was the hapless former owner. Besides the obvious reasons for upholding the law, there is a very important practical reason. If you provide a creditor with an unauthorized "sweetener," you can be sure that others will find about it through leaks in your company or otherwise, and on what grounds can you then refuse equalizer payments to them? So, when those phone calls start—just say "no."

When those former creditors contact you, that creates a perfect opportunity to mend the company's relationship with them. While being careful to deflect their requests for direct or indirect payments of the discharged debts, through your sympathetic response you might dissipate their anger. Then you may be able to persuade them to reinstitute sales on credit to the company. In this matter you may be able to bring important suppliers back into the fold.

Aside from following the plan requirements, probably the most important thing that you can do is to continually update and follow the business plan you used to focus on the company as a good turnaround candidate. Do not allow the euphoria of the acquisition cause you to forget the urgent tasks that must be accomplished. New patterns must be established quickly, in the order dictated by your prior determination of the Critical Path. Income must be produced, and expenses kept in line, according to your cash flow projection. The corporate culture of unprofitability and disorganization must be replaced by one of success and controlled growth.

So, you are off and running. Good luck, but remember that if things do not go as you had hoped, there is always Chapter 11!

Part III

BUYING OUT OF CHAPTER 7

Chapter 14

The Chapter 7 Process

A company can become a Chapter 7 Debtor in one of three ways. It may file a voluntary petition asking to be liquidated pursuant to that chapter. It may be placed involuntarily into bankruptcy by any three creditors whose claims together total at least five thousand dollars and it may respond by choosing to undergo Chapter 7 liquidation rather than attempting Chapter 11 reorganization. It may have failed to reorganize under Chapter 11, and suffered a conversion of its case by the bankruptcy judge to that under Chapter 7.

Upon the entry of an order determining a party to be a Debtor under Chapter 7, the United States Trustee names a trustee to administer any assets. In the case of a voluntary Chapter 7 filing, that order is deemed to have been entered automatically, without the necessity of any action from a judge, instantaneously upon the filing of the bankruptcy petition with the bankruptcy court clerk—another one of the law's "little white fictions." In most cases, the trustee is picked from a standing list of screened, qualified candidates. In very large, politically sensitive, or complicated cases the United States Trustee may bypass the panel in choosing a trustee. (Yes, that means that in very lucrative cases the trustee is likely to be someone who knows very little about bankruptcy but has great connections with the U.S. Trustee in that district. This lucky person then hires a well-connected bankruptcy attorney to act as his lawyer and keep him out of trouble. Did I ever say that life in bankruptcy court was different than life in the Real World?)

In the case of a business Debtor with assets to protect, the process must move quickly. The U.S. Trustee's office usually acts expeditiously in notifying the trustee of his appointment. If the U.S. Trustee's office is aware of any special problems, such as perishable commodities or stores not yet closed, it will advise the trustee. The trustee must "batten the hatches" as soon as possible.

As a former trustee, I can attest to the panic engendered by the telephone call that informs the trustee that he is now responsible for gaining control over a messy situation. For example, I have been appointed as trustee of: a grocery store stocked with rapidly rotting meat, vegetables, and fruit, with the city health department governing my sale of the produce; a slum apartment with more than one hundred units, for which I was expected to collect the rents and keep the tenants from dumping their garbage out their windows; an entire, operating shopping center, with a leaky roof and a parking lot with potholes the size of cars; and more other horror stories than I care to think about. I know one thing: show me an experienced bankruptcy trustee, and I will show you a person who carries the telephone numbers of a locksmith available at any time of day or night, a board-up service, and the police!

Securing the assets also runs to the intangibles. Bank accounts must be frozen, utility service must be continued or restored (especially heat during the winter—frozen water pipes can easily burst and flood a building), and customer lists and other proprietary data must be retained and protected. The trustee must be added as a party in interest to any insurance still in force. Etc., etc., etc.

Once the assets of the bankruptcy estate are secured, the trustee can then turn his attention to liquidating them. If the Debtor is an individual, the first step is to determine which personal and household assets remain the Debtor's and are "exempt" from being administered by the trustee. However, generally speaking, business assets are not accorded exemptions.

The first step in liquidating assets of a Chapter 7 Debtor is to review the liens that the secured creditors claim to hold. The trustee must review all relevant documents and informally question the Debtor and each lienholder to acquire sufficient information to form an opinion of the validity of each lien, which property of the Debtor serves as collateral, and the amount of the secured creditor's claim.

While most liens pass muster, in a significant percentage of cases the trustee asks the bankruptcy judge to rule on some aspect of the lien claim. For reasons explained later, the trustee has a good deal of incentive to challenge lien claims that appear vulnerable.

The trustee next must form an opinion about the likely liquidation value of the Debtor's property that serves as security for each lien. Most of the time the trustee's valuation is more of a guess than anything else, formulated after hearing the wildly differing views of the owner of the Debtor, the lienholder, and the major trade creditors. Where there is a substantial amount of machinery and equipment, an appraiser or professional liquidator may be retained to give a formal opinion.

The point of the process is to set the likely proceeds from the sale of the collateral (net, after subtracting expenses of the sale) against that amount of the valid lien claims secured by that collateral, to see which is greater. If the likely net proceeds exceed the secured creditors' claims, there is said to be "equity for the estate," and the trustee will sell the collateral, pay the secured claims in full, pay his expenses of the sale, and place the remaining funds into his trustee's bank account. If the amount of the secured claims against the collateral exceeds the likely net proceeds, there is no equity in those assets and theoretically the secured creditors have the right to take the collateral away from the estate. (In most cases, there will be only one lien upon an asset, and so for convenience from now on I will generally refer to "the secured creditor" or "the lienholder.")

Since the trustee cannot force the secured creditor to acquiesce to a sale of collateral that will probably not produce equity for the estate, the secured creditor controls the method of liquidation. Most of the time the secured lender will choose to take possession of the collateral and will hold a foreclosure sale pursuant to state law. Occasionally, a secured creditor will permit the trustee to place the assets for sale, either because the price will be increased by being part of the trustee's sale or because the secured creditor does not wish to bother holding a sale. However, because the trustee earns a fee—paid by the secured creditor—for holding such a sale, leading some trustees to pressure secured creditors to permit such a sale, a number of bankruptcy judges around the country will not permit trustees in cases before them to sell assets unless the sale almost certainly will produce funds for the estate.

It is not uncommon for all of the assets of a Chapter 7 company to be subject to a "blanket lien" of a bank. In that case, the question of who liquidates the assets is important to the unsecured creditors since it is generally felt that a court-supervised sale is more likely to produce equity for them. The issue is *crucial* to the trustee because if all of the assets are turned over to the bank, he will receive no fee for administering them, in spite of expending time on the many duties associated with the case.

As you might expect, trustees and secured creditors frequently are in dispute over the valuation of assets and the validity and amount of secured claims. The trustees may require the secured creditor to prove its claim in a hearing before the bankruptcy judge, or the creditor may file a motion to request such a determination if the trustee indicates that he will not recognize the lien. One of the parties in interest may ask the court to rule upon the valuation of the collateral, in order to determine the trustee's right to sell the assets; however, since such hearings are summary in nature, the court's findings usually amount to not much more than a semi-educated guess. In any event, as you can see, the system provides for processes to thrash out the issues and to liquidate assets that are subject to liens.

The trustee then commences to convert all of the noncash property of the estate to cash by selling it. The assets may be sold at a "public sale"—an auction—or at a "private sale." Property that cannot be sold after reasonable efforts is abandoned.

After the estate is reduced to cash and the validity and the extent of the claims have been determined, the case can be closed. The trustee files a report that describes what he did, the amount of cash in the estate, and the amounts and classes of the various claims. After the U.S. Trustee's office and the bankruptcy court clerk's office review the report to make sure that the trustee has fulfilled his duties and has not made any errors or omissions in it, a final hearing before the bankruptcy judge is scheduled on notice to all parties in interest.

The final hearing usually is perfunctory, with the court approving the report without much comment. While it is possible for creditors to object to any element of the trustee's administration of the case, in practice all of the fights have already been fought. The major item of business at the hearing is the final award of the trustee's commission and the fees for the trustee's attorneys and accountants, which occasionally provokes some sparks in the courtroom. Whether or not there is any objection to the requested commission and fees, the bankruptcy judge will exercise his prerogative to scrutinize the requests and may cut them.

Once the court determines the amount of the commission and the fees, grants the trustee reimbursement of his expenses directly associated with the administration of the case, and approves the final report, the trustee may disburse the funds of the estate. The trustee writes checks to pay the costs of administration as allowed, and to pay the creditors according to their respective places on the hierarchy established by the bankruptcy code. Needless to say, the percentage paid upon unsecured claims is usually very much less than one hundred and very little more than zero.

Once it is established that the trustee has assets to administer, if they have any significant value, the trustee moves to sell them.

The most common situation is for the trustee to schedule one auction sale for all of the assets of the Debtor. Thus not only will the physical assets be put up for bid, but the trustee will also offer patent rights, trademarks, customer lists, and goodwill (including the right to use the business' name). Trustees usually try to avoid piecemeal sales of the assets.

If there are a substantial number of physical assets to be sold, most likely the trustee will retain the services of an auctioneer. Trustees ordinarily lack the staff and the desire to accomplish all of the work of cataloguing the individual items of machinery, equipment, furniture, and supplies, and holding showings prior to the sale. Also, trustees generally prefer to have an experienced auctioneer handle the auction itself, which can easily get out of control if attended by experienced liquidators jockeying for every possible advantage. The auctioneer may also agree to cart away any unsold items. For his services, the auctioneer is paid a percentage commission (which almost always exceeds the trustee's commission) plus expenses.

The auction sale must be advertised. Many federal districts have rules respecting the minimum requirements for providing public notice. Trustees also tend to follow local custom as to the form and placement of newspaper ads, such as using special sections for the advertisement of auction sales contained in many newspapers. It is rare for a trustee to extend his advertising efforts beyond the minimal regular and customary means.

Whether by custom or local rule, most advertisements give a generic description of the items to be auctioned (e.g., "machinery and equipment utilized in the manufacture of drill bits, heat treating equipment, two forklift trucks, and miscellaneous office furniture, equipment and supplies"); the date, time, and place of the auction sale; the dates and times during which the property to be auctioned may be inspected, and the location of the property; and special terms of the sale, such as the percentage of any successful bid that must be deposited by certified or cashier's check on the date of the sale, requirements for removing items purchased, etc.

In addition to providing some opportunity to view the items to be offered at auction, the trustee is supposed to respond to inquiries and requests for information. The major problem is that the trustee is usually fairly ignorant about the items that he will be putting up for sale and almost never has anything useful to say. Also, while not usually unfriendly, the trustee has little time or attention for the many telephone inquiries that the ads produce. The system is not made for amateur bidders.

If an auctioneer has been retained, he may be more helpful than the trustee. He will be more comfortable talking with prospective bidders. Oftentimes, the auctioneer is also a liquidator and dealer in used machinery and equipment and so may provide real insight into the items being offered for sale.

Ordinarily, inspections by prospective bidders are limited in date, time, and scope. Trustees and auctioneers are usually not inclined to make exceptions, to allow either a private inspection or an inspection that results in any items being taken apart or otherwise fooled with. Prospective bidders are expected to conform to the dates and times and make a rather cursory inspection of the items to be auctioned.

Whether the trustee or the auctioneer will be holding the auction, often there are rules that the bidders will be required to follow, but are not clearly expressed in the advertisements or at the inspections. Sometimes each prospective bidder that attends the auction is required to leave a certain amount in a cashier's or certified check at the door as security for the bidder's performance of any successful bids, breakage, or conduct which may hinder the sale of any item. At other times, it only may be required that a prospective bidder have in his possession a sufficient sum in cashier's or certified checks to pay a fixed percentage (usually ten percent) of the purchase price of any item immediately on the conclusion of the bidding. Auction sales vary greatly in the amount of time that a successful bidder has to pay for the purchased item in full, but it is usually *short*—sometimes *very short*. The deadline for removing purchased items may be only a day or two. As you gain experience, you will develop a list of issues to which you will seek answers prior to the sale date.

Because an auction is such a hurry-up process, there simply is no time for a bidder to arrange financing after being assured of the high bid. Neither the trustee nor the auctioneer will stand for a bidder who says he needs a week to secure a loan to pay for the goods. As a result, a prospective bidder must either have cash in the bank or arrange for a line of credit ahead of time in the likely amount of purchases.

The auction sale itself moves very quickly. An experienced trustee or auctioneer will want to maintain tight control over the proceedings, which generally means moving rapidly from item to item and not allowing the bidders to cause problems with demands or tricky questions. At larger sales, the auctioneer may move about on a wheeled pedestal, always in position to start the bidding on the next item. Bidders do not have much time to think or bid. The least likely request to be granted is: "Could you hold up bidding for five minutes while I call my office for authority to bid higher?"

It may seem strange that the auction procedures are not more forgiving, to encourage more bidding and higher bids, but anyone who has chaired an auction will tell you that the biggest problem is maintaining control. The problem becomes acute at the larger sales, with the ranks of prospective bidders filled with sharp, pushy, competitive, professional used-equipment dealers who may have as much or more auction experience than the person holding the auction.

The identity of each successful bidder and the amount of each winning bid will be recorded carefully. If no deposit was required prior to the commencement of the auction, the successful bidder may be asked to step up and pay the minimum deposit immediately at the conclusion of the bidding and to provide personal or company information to establish identity unless a registration process was completed prior to the bidding. A winning bidder who fails to comply with the auction sales most certainly will lose his deposit and may be sued by the trustee for the deficiency if the item cannot be resold at the same price.

Whether by custom or local court rule, commonly the trustee solicits offers for a "bulk bid" at the conclusion of the bidding for individual items. If the highest bulk bid exceeds the sum of the winning bids for individual items, the successful bulk bidder comes away with all of the property that was for sale. Obviously this is a great opportunity for a determined bidder to come away with an intact production line.

With very rare exceptions, property is sold at auction "AS IS," with no warranties or representations of any kind. Prospective bidders are expected to make their own inspections, do their own research respecting machinery and equipment capabilities, and otherwise do their "homework." Trustees are petrified of product liability problems, not only because a successful claim made during the course of the case might decimate the bankruptcy estate but also because a claim prosecuted after he has disbursed the funds of the estate and closed the case might result in his personal liability. (One of the favorite games of the experienced bidders is to try to get the trustee or auctioneer to say something—anything—about the items offered for sale that may be used to void the sale later if any piece of machinery turns out to be a lemon.) The "AS IS" nature of the auction sale applies whether the item sold is a stamping machine, truck, customer list, or corporate name.

While, of course, there is increased risk in buying property from a know-nothing seller such as a trustee, in general it is balanced by a lower purchase price. In other words, the price generally reflects all of the factors of the forced sale. The buyer who has a definitive use for the auction property, whether to expand an operation or commence a new business, can be confident that he has paid the lowest price and has set the stage for profits that can be a megamultiple of invested capital. That is what makes auction sales so attractive to the quick and the clever.

While auction sales are preferred because they are less subject to abuse, some assets of an estate may be disposed of at a private sale— that is, upon an arrangement between the trustee and a third party, arrived at through their negotiations and not as a result of competitive bidding.

The most likely items to be sold at private sale are those that are rapidly perishing or diminishing in value. The theory is that by the time an auction can be scheduled, advertised, and held, the assets will bring in significantly less than even the heavily discounted price no doubt negotiated by a private buyer. This is another opportunity for a prospective purchaser who is waiting in the wings and who has immediate use for the items. Good timing, perhaps prompted by a quick inquiry to the trustee shortly after his appointment, can be rewarded.

The trustee is required to seek prior court approval of the private sale. The trustee must persuade the bankruptcy judge that the situation warrants an emergency sale and that he has made an attempt to achieve a price reasonable under the circumstances. For example, he may show the judge that he solicited offers from three different likely buyers. (In the case mentioned earlier in which I was appointed trustee of a grocery store, I sold the inventory that the health department cleared to another grocery store within three days of being appointed trustee.)

Trustees are constantly being asked by prospective buyers to sell nonperishable items at private sale, but only foolish trustees will do so. The experienced trustee will be afraid of being criticized for a private sale; besides, that prospective purchaser will most likely be willing to bid at least the proffered amount at any auction, and so refusing to make a private sale will result in no loss to the estate. Need I say that offering a "private" inducement to a trustee to facilitate a private sale is a federal no-no?

Another category of item sold at private sale is that for which there is a recognized market, as characterized by public, quoted prices. Sale of those items through the regular market process is both inexpensive for the estate and provides little chance of trustee abuse. Items sold in this manner include stocks sold through exchanges or "over the counter," stamp and coin collections, and commodities. Because automobiles, trucks, and trailers have fairly standardized values that are reported in listings used throughout the industry, those types of assets are often sold by the trustee to a dealer for the generally recognized wholesale value.

Real estate is a hybrid. While one cannot simply consult a manual or a published quotation for a price—because, in theory, every piece of real estate is unique—the fair market value of most parcels of real estate can be determined within a reasonable range. In fact, a formal appraisal of real estate by a certified appraiser amounts, more or less, to a market quote. Accordingly, if management of the parcel is not burdensome to the trustee, the trustee may place it for sale through a real-estate broker rather than upon auction. Because the listed property is not being offered at a forced sale and because of the professional services provided by the broker, it is assumed that the net proceeds after paying the broker's commission will still exceed the likely proceeds from an auction. However, if an auction sale is given reasonable publicity, a trustee generally will not be criticized for auctioning real estate that could have been sold through a broker.

Distressed real estate is generally sold at auction. Rental property that is losing money, buildings that are unsafe, property that is not insurable, etc., are quickly disposed of at auction. Parcels that a broker has been unable to sell within a reasonable time are offered at auction.

Buying real estate from a bankruptcy trustee can be a real bargain for the knowledgeable buyer. Although parcels offered through a broker should theoretically be sold at a "market price," a trustee is usually happy to receive an offer at the low end of the market price range. Also, a trustee is not a patient seller and will often jump at a low-ball price if the property has not sold quite as quickly as expected. The trustee may view as serious threats problems that an experienced property manager could easily take care of. (The trustee may have hired a professional property manager, but no doubt goes into panic when he hears of burst pipes, required furnace repairs, etc.). The natural result of the trustee system is to produce a very good deal for the buyer from the estate.

As described earlier, if the likely proceeds from the sale of property of the estate subject to a lien will not exceed the amount of the lien claim, the trustee may simply turn the collateral over to the secured creditor, usually a bank.

The bank's liquidation of the collateral is very similar to the trustee's methods. While the bank adheres to state laws respecting the foreclosure of personal property (the Uniform Commercial Code) and real estate (mortgage foreclosure statutes) instead of federal bankruptcy law, in general the bank is required to offer the property for sale upon fair public notice. Consequently, buying from the bank is very similar to buying from the trustee. In fact, in the case of substantial business assets, the process of buying from the bank may be identical to buying from a trustee in that both are likely to auction the property using the services of an auctioneer.

The bank faces the same pressures and concerns as the trustee. The bank may be loathe to hold the property for any substantial length of time and may fear the potential liability inherent in being responsible for it. It is less interested in getting the top dollar for the property than in getting rid of it. It will follow at least the minimal requirements for advertisement, etc., because it does not want to get sued by the borrower. For the same reason, it probably will not sell at private sale unless there is some emergency—although I have found bankers somewhat more willing to do so than trustees, whether out of bravado or ignorance.

The prospective buyers should approach the bank in a similar manner as contacting a trustee. First and foremost, information respecting the manner and rules of the sale should be carefully noted and followed. During the course of those discussions, it can be determined how much leeway there is in the bank's proposed procedures, and whether it can be persuaded to hold a quick private sale in bulk to you. While such a sale may not necessarily be in the bank's best interest, it just might do it. It never hurts to ask!

Chapter 15

Why Buy Out of Chapter 7?

Let me reemphasize that the best way to acquire a new business is to buy an operating company out of Chapter 11. There are many benefits to taking over a company that is already up and running, and ordinarily the price is quite reasonable when compared to the sums demanded for profitable companies. However, certain other goals may be met quite well by buying the pieces of a closed business out of Chapter 7.

It is a real confidence builder to see a competitor's company liquidated, and the opportunity to cherry-pick a former competitor's assets is an opportunity too good to refuse. It is a chance to add to existing production capacity, and/or replace dottering machinery. Customer lists and other trade secrets also should be available. Buying out of Chapter 7 allows the survivor not only to benefit indirectly from the fact that there is one less competitor out there, but also to benefit directly through the acquisition of its assets. It is an invitation to Instant Expansion!

In such a situation, what may be too high a price for liquidators and other visitors to the auction will still amount to a "steal" for the bidder who is already in the same business. Consequently, through determined bidding on the individual items, and perhaps bidding upon the "bulk" sale in a manner that shows an unstoppable attitude, the other bidders may get discouraged and a foundation for a much larger business can be laid. Even if the prices have been driven up through competitive bidding, they still will be only a fraction of the cost (both in time and money) that otherwise would be required to achieve such an expansion of your business.

Another possible goal in buying out of Chapter 7 is to deal in the machinery, equipment, and furniture of the Debtor. While requiring a solid knowledge of the markets, used business items are in constant demand and large profits can be made buying cheaply at a Chapter 7 and quickly "turning over" the items to buyers in private sales. Sometimes a sharp operator will even know how to turn over intangibles such as customer lists and patent rights.

Dealing in assets of defunct companies is somewhat like being an arbitrager on the stock market—it is not for the fainthearted. Much energy must be expanded in buying right and selling right, and the need for sharp appraisal abilities and sound judgment is paramount. However, the rewards can be huge.

Of course, a hybrid approach can prove profitable in two ways. By buying assets to blend in with an ongoing operation or to expand, a purchaser also may end up with unwanted used machinery and equipment. The purchaser's older machinery and equipment may be looking for a new home, and/or perhaps some of the newly purchased items do not work out. If the buyer has done a good job, the new equipment alone will be worth the expense, and the sale of the other pieces on the used machinery and equipment market will provide the "frosting on the cake."

The third goal of buying out of Chapter 7 is perhaps the riskiest— attempting to enter into a new business by resurrecting the company. This path requires a person with a lot of confidence, time, energy, and a burning desire to start a business at the lowest possible cost.

Some circumstances can serve to decrease the risk. Perhaps the buyer is already an employee of a competing company and can quickly infuse customers and experienced personnel. Perhaps the company has been liquidated during an off-season for its products, and so few if any customers have been lost. In other words, the business may need only the "kiss" of a "prince" to come alive again.

You may be someone who does not need especially favorable circumstances. You simply may desire to maximize the "bang for your buck" in starting a new business. You may prefer to construct your own production line and hire your own employees than come into a situation with such things already decided by someone else. If so, and you are right, your return upon invested capital can be a percentage too large to print on this page!

An analogy can be drawn between buying a company out of Chapter 7 and privateering of days gone by.

A major reason for England's rise as a sea power was the willingness of the monarchy to make "privateers" out of "pirates."

There was a slew of English pirates who showed no discrimination in their conquests, robbing English ships as well as those of England's competitors, Spain, France, and Holland. When captured by the Royal Navy, they were executed. The English government preferred not to kill some of its most aggressive, able seamen; and the marauders were none too pleased about having their necks stretched. Why not cut a deal that would benefit both sides?

The arrangement was simple: the pirates agreed to spare English vessels, and the English government declared them to be "privateers" engaged in "commerce." They were protected from the force of English law because their booty from other countries' ships was declared by the English government to be legally acquired. Their activities suddenly became legal, even desirable.

Chapter 7 allows asset purchasers to be legal "privateers." The goods may be acquired at immorally low prices and may be sold again through private channels very quickly. The best items may be "cherry-picked," leaving others to struggle with the remains. The acquisition process is quick and takes every advantage of the holder of the assets. The acquirer takes giant steps up over the supine form of the provider. And it is legal.

Privateering in Chapter 7 certainly has its thrills. There are huge numbers of business assets being administered by the bankruptcy courts from which to choose. If prices are too high at any particular auction, the smart buyer simply waits for the next. When assets for sale would be *very* useful, they can be acquired in a lightning strike. The result can be great riches.

However, even legal privateers must be aware of the dangers.

The system has built-in pitfalls. The "booty" may turn out to be "fools' gold" and "costume jewelry." Pieces of equipment may not work right, and the customer base may have fled. Whether through overbidding or because of a failure to produce profits, the assets were overpriced. It is not surprising that losses can result because the "upside" can be so great. Face it—where there is opportunity for great profits, there is great risk and thus chance for loss.

However, risks can be minimized through hard work, competence, good timing, and sound judgment. If you feel that you have those qualities, you just may strike it rich in bankruptcy court!

Chapter 16

How to Buy at Auction

Since auction sales to be held by either bankruptcy trustees or banks must be advertised, a little searching through local newspapers will lead you to the customary places for such notices. They may be in the classified ad section, in the business section, or on some other page in their own "Auction Sales" section. The specially dedicated section may only run once a week, commonly in the most popular edition, for example, the Sunday edition of the local general circulation newspaper.

Substantial auction sales may be given wider publicity. Ads may be placed in "national" newspapers such as the *Wall Street Journal* and *The New York Times,* and/or national trade magazines. If there is a widely read local business weekly, ads may be placed there.

While it is useful to maintain a watch over likely spots for auction sale notices, it always helps to have a trustee contact you directly. Personal notice avoids the problem of missing an ad and may allow for additional preparation time.

To get on trustees' personal notice lists, you should write to them. First contact the United States Trustee for each federal district that is convenient to you and ask for a list of the Chapter 7 panel trustees. Then send each trustee a form letter asking that you be notified directly of asset sales, and, if you wish, indicating the type of assets in which you are interested in purchasing. Do not expect a rousing response, but most regular trustees will stash your letter in a file of liquidators and others who request notice of sales. After all, you just might help him out sometime by taking a "difficult" asset off of his hands.

Some United States Trustee's offices and local bankruptcy court clerks keep a public list of scheduled trustee sales. Telephone to find out if such lists exist. Use any such list as only a backup, as they are often not up-to-date.

As for bank sales, whether resulting from Chapter 7 liquidations or Uniform Commercial Code foreclosures, similar procedures can be followed. The bank foreclosure notices will be found in the same places as the trustee notices. Similar letters can be sent to the departments in the larger local banks that deal with distressed loans.

You no doubt have many ideas about how to get those assets under liquidation as easily as possible and as quickly as possible. You are focused on your own needs and wants. However, if you pause for a bit and try to look at the case through the eyes of the trustee, you will gain insight into how to deal with him.

First and foremost, the trustee depends upon his relations with the office of the United States Trustee, and indirectly upon his relations with the bankruptcy judges, in his federal district to assure a steady flow of trustee assignments. The trustee is expected to administer cases in a *quiet,* competent manner that does not cause disputes that must be heard by the court. He is expected to know and follow the law in liquidating the estate, especially the local rules in many districts that specify procedures for liquidating assets and holding sales.

It does *not* disturb those relations if the trustee, in following the bare minimum requirements of the sales, fails to maximize the potential proceeds from the sale of assets. In effect, the trustee is rewarded for unexceptional performance; or, as I often characterize it, trustees are not paid to be heroes.

Another major factor is that the trustee's maximum commission is set at:

15 percent of the first $1,000;

6 percent of the next $2,000; and

3 percent of any excess;

upon all monies handled by the trustee. (The bankruptcy judge in each case is free to award a *lesser* fee, and many do so quite frequently.) Considering the many administrative tasks that the trustee is supposed to do, the commission rarely amounts to a substantial hourly rate or amount. For example, it almost never approaches attorneys' fees in the same cases. (In fact, most trustees are bankruptcy attorneys who do their own legal work, and thus make the majority of their income as attorneys.) Except for the business cases with substantial assets to turn into cash, the trustees' fees are quite modest.

Because the commission percentage is so small, there is not that much incentive to increase the proceeds of sales. Therefore, most trustees show not the slightest interest in marketing the assets in a businesslike manner or otherwise acting above and beyond the call of duty.

Another reason why trustees do not market their wares better is: fear. Considering their rather modest commissions, trustees have a lot of responsibility. Assets separated from their owners tend to disappear. Former employees of the defunct company take their revenge. No one seems to know where the right keys are or who else has copies. Commonly the insurance policies have been cancelled. Therefore, the trustee's primary goal is to *get rid of the stuff* before it disappears in a way that will subject the trustee to criticism by the creditors, U.S. Trustee, and/or the bankruptcy judge. Consequently, the auction process is almost always expedited.

The trustee is also afraid of taking some innovative action to increase the sales proceeds that backfires. A business executive recognizes that something less than one hundred percent of his bright ideas will work, but there is no provision in the bankruptcy process to average out the successes and failures of separate cases. A trustee who has failed in even a modestly risky course of action may find his commission cancelled and himself "surcharged," that is, forced to pay damages to the creditors.

Trustees also have a Fear of Favoritism, at least if it is so obvious it leaves the trustee open to criticism. Trustees are not above giving their friends advance notice and viewing of assets that will be coming up for sale, because if it comes to light such actions can be defended as "increasing the numbers of bidders." However, one should not expect a trustee to readily accept an offer to buy the assets at a private no-bid sale unless circumstances clearly warrant it, because such a method of sale smacks of favoritism *that costs the estate money* and rationales for its use are likely to be treated with skepticism by the creditors, U.S. Trustee, and the judge. (Not surprisingly, conspiring with the trustee to deny other interested parties a fair chance to bid for the assets is a federal crime.)

The primary result of these concerns of the trustee is to produce a liquidation process limited by express rules and implied local customs to a relatively standard format. Accordingly, the most important thing you should do is to learn those parameters and be ready to act within them. Your brilliant maneuvers may go unmaneuvered, but at least trustees will love you because you do not cause them trouble and because you take assets off their hands.

Get the facts—fast.

Because of the concerns of the trustees, usually time is of the essence in auction sales. The time between the first public notice and the date of the sale often is quite short, sometimes only a manner of weeks. Consequently, you must be really on the ball and have a fast reaction time to play this game.

You should attempt to reach the trustee by telephone to fill in the gaps in the notice. You will impress the trustee if you have a list of concise, targeted questions that show him that you are not wasting his time. First ask about the procedural details concerning the inspection of assets, bidding at the auction, and removal of purchased items. Find out if a listing of the assets exists, and, if so, whether the trustee will allow you to view it, allow you to pick up a copy, or mail a copy to you. Only after you have covered the specific information requirements should you try to draw out comment from the trustee on the nature of the assets for sale.

"Kick the tires" as much as possible. Spend as much time inspecting the physical assets as you can, even if part of the time is spent hanging around listening to other people's comments. Telephone friends and business associates who might be able to provide some insight into the machinery and equipment that is for sale. See if the books, records, and other business papers in the hands of the trustee contain any information. Look for warranty registrations, bills of sale, maintenance history, and operating manuals. (The trustee will be happy to have you search for those items, which will benefit his sale if you are a good guy and show him what you find.)

While it may seem indelicate, you might telephone the former owner or employees of the defunct company. The owner may very well be a guarantor on the bank loan to the company and may be interested in providing information to maximize the sale proceeds. Former employees may feel that a job opportunity has arisen; in any event, you are sure to hear "the dirt" about the way the company was operated.

As you can see, learning about the assets for sale is dependent almost entirely on your own initiative and determination. If you expect to be in a position to use sound judgment on auction day, you must do your "homework" thoroughly beforehand.

By auction day you should know on what you want to bid, the maximum bid that you can and will make for each such item, and how to effectuate any winning bid. All open issues and procedures should have been determined beforehand. You should have taken full advantage of your inspection rights and thoroughly researched the assets for sale. If you have not accomplished all of these things, do not bid.

Money talks, but you have to use the right language to be understood. For the safety of both the trustee and you, do not carry large amounts of cash. (At one of my trustee sales, a bidder's pocket was picked of several thousand dollars.) Bring cashier's or certified checks only. Be sure to have checks totalling the exact amount of any required deposit, as the trustee is in no position to make change at the auction. The secret is to have a number of checks in varying incremental amounts that can be shuffled to produce an exact total. Checks should be made out to the trustee, or made out to you and signed over to the trustee with a limited endorsement in the event you are required to make a deposit.

Arrive early, and get the "lay of the land." Listen to comments by the liquidators and other prospective bidders. Not only might you learn more about the property for sale, but you might also make some useful business contacts and learn of possible purchasers of any machinery or equipment that you later spin off. (However, be advised: agreeing with other prospective bidders to limit competitive bidding in any way at a bankruptcy auction is a federal crime.)

Know the rules of the auction. Clarify any uncertainties before the bidding begins. Listen to questions by other prospective bidders. Be prepared to follow those rules—at least until you become experienced enough to know how and when they bend!

Be a smart bidder. If you have partners or are financing any successful bids, know the limits of your bidding authority, as it will not be possible to get a recess during bidding to make a telephone call. In addition to knowing how much you *can* bid, for each item set a maximum amount that you *will* bid AND STICK TO IT. I have found that competitive bidding for desirable assets often produces a final price that is no bargain.

Experience helps. Attend some auctions first at which you do not plan to bid at all, just to get the feel of the process. Do not try for the "big kill" on your first several outings. Learn from those more experienced than you.

In conclusion, buying out of auction can produce large returns, and so the risks are great. It is not something to be done without the investment of your valuable time. However, if you are methodical, learn the express rules and implied customs, and do not get carried

away in your bidding, you will be well rewarded through your
participation in the process.

PART IV

CONCLUSION

Chapter 17

Finding the Right Fit

The strategies described in this book work. They are not based upon an arcane trick that will become useless as soon as it is generally known. They do, however, require personal initiative, business sense, and a knowledge of the rules and customs of the game.

Because buying bankrupt companies is not done through gimmicks, I cannot promise you guaranteed, unbridled success on every outing. One reason is that, while it probably is not any harder to buy a bankrupt company than to buy a profitable business, then again it is probably not any easier either! Whether through court or through a private market, the majority of attempts at acquiring a company do not achieve fruition.

In many cases, the investigation will lead the prospective purchaser to conclude that he does not wish to make an offer. Such a decision may be based upon a negative finding respecting any number of important factors, many of which have been touched upon in this book. Perhaps a thorough investigation of the target company disclosed that the likely benefits of the acquisition will not merit the capital and/or time required, at least for that prospective purchaser. Perhaps the target company cannot be saved. For another example, when investigating a company in an unfamiliar industry, what the prospective buyer may learn is that he really does not want to be in that industry. In those situations the proper action is to "walk away," and the prospective purchaser should not feel any duty to consummate a deal.

A major factor that derails acquisitions is a mismatch in "time" or "place." The prospective buyer just may not be ready to do the deal—his money may be tied up elsewhere, he is completing another acquisition, he has production problems at his own company, etc. Sometimes it is the seller who throws off the timing by delaying matters until the company is seriously slumping or out of credit. Sometimes the parties simply cannot arrange their schedules to sit down and talk. In the meantime, the "window of opportunity" gets boarded up.

Some of the failure to find a fit has a subjective element, rather than a factual, objective basis. Egos may clash. One side or the other may overplay its hand and sour the negotiations—not an uncommon occurrence in the high-stakes acquisitions game. While ideally subjective factors can be isolated and bypassed, in the Real World, they can easily overshadow cold, hard facts. (I do not consider the intuitive feeling that a deal is "not right" to be purely subjective, if that feeling arises from a thorough investigation into the target company. It probably constitutes a very logical, rational conclusion based upon many pieces of evidence.)

The attitude and general psychological outlook of the prospective purchaser can have a lot to do with whether he sees a "fit" in any given situation. Business acquisitions in general, and acquiring bankrupt companies in particular, require an optimist at the helm. Pessimists do not become rich.

The kind of optimism I am talking about is not the naiveté of a Pollyanna that says that everything is all right, no matter what (an ultimate form of subjectivity). It is an attitude that most problems can be solved and improvements can be accomplished. It is founded upon a confidence in oneself, and a positive, uncynical mind set. True optimists have a way of overcoming inertia, of making things happen, that "prudent" people would not think to attempt.

An optimistic, "can-do" attitude is a prerequisite to acquiring bankrupt companies. *The essence of buying out of bankruptcy is that the companies are only as good as what buyers will do with them.* They are obviously unprofitable, and their recent history is poor. The pessimist will focus on what has been and what is—the status quo—rather than what can be. He will never take the leap, he will never make an offer. (He should become a banker.) The optimist will focus on the company as it will be and will set about making that vision into reality.

One should always be on the lookout for negative, "can't-do" attitudes that pose as prudence. For example, I do not subscribe to the adage that advises: it is better to walk away from nine good deals than to make one bad deal. To me, it smacks of blind caution, which is nothing more than another ultimate form of subjectivity. It speaks of an inability to discern a good deal from a bad one. I prefer to counsel educated, intelligent, *decision-making,* and competent management skills, which will lead to homing in on the good deals and minimizing the effects of the few errors in judgment that must occur.

If one has both patience and confidence, the issues become more defined, the answers clearer. It becomes easier to find one's way through the thicket of possibilities, avoiding the pitfalls and focusing on the true opportunities. When the spotlight falls upon the right choice—when the right fit presents itself—the way to seize the initiative and close the acquisition becomes almost obvious.

And you will find the right fit because the field is wide open.

It may be said that the bankruptcy courts are the primary market for companies and business assets for sale in this country, and yet the process is barely touched by prospective purchasers. There are many good companies to choose from in Chapter 11, and huge amounts of business assets for sale in Chapter 7 every year. Bankruptcy court holds the opportunities that you are searching for and those that you will be surprised to find.

To summarize this chapter, there are many good and bad reasons why an acquisition is not effectuated, and one should not expect a majority of possible deals to fall into place. Consequently, one must have patience and fortitude in the search. One must break off the pursuit of a target that proves not worthy and rebound from the failure to capture a prize dearly sought, without tiring of the chase. Why? Because somewhere out there are companies that can provide you with the riches of which you dream.

Chapter 18

Replication and Riches

It is possible to make a lot of money operating one small business. The owner can be quite satisfied to head a profitable company and make a good living. However, some people are not satisfied with that comfortable state of affairs, and they may have good reasons.

First and foremost, while starting a business is very difficult and takes many years to reach an adequate size, acquiring a company allows for a rapid entry into a market. That is why the trend in business economics during the 1980s and for the foreseeable future is toward expansion through acquisition.

The tools are all in place to grow through acquisitions. Computerization and management methods have progressed to the point where multiple entities are not harder to control than a single unit, and in fact bring economies of scale to bear. Institutional lenders have been shown the way and are now quite comfortable—eager, even—to fund purchases of entire companies.

While the business history books provide us with examples of corporate empires that have crashed due to unwise overexpansion, the lessons respecting that "domino effect" need to be updated because business executives of today are more able to turn size and complexity to their favor. Conglomerates offer a hedge against adversity in any one business. Managerial and financial assets can be shifted among the units. More and better executives can be nurtured. Complexity can screen internal problems from outside observers (including creditors), who often cannot understand enough about the operation to be able to tell when it is having difficulties.

As a bankruptcy lawyer, I have become acutely aware that the more pieces an organization has, the more interrelationships (and manipulation) that exist within the structure, and the larger the work force, the *less* likely it is that it will be closed and liquidated. Creditors are unwilling to be the cause of the demise of a conglomerate, even if they know how to attack it. Bankruptcy judges give more deference to the executives of conglomerates. Because of the desire on the part of all the interests to keep big companies going, in the really large multicorporate bankruptcies, the Debtor totally dominate and control the cases.

The general lesson to be learned from these trends is that acquiring companies offers a sound method for building *and keeping* riches.

Another reason why many business owners are not satisfied to merely maintain the status quo is that their personalities will not let them. The good executives are always looking for the next challenge. They are confident not only in their ability to vanquish the beast but also that in triumphing, they will add to their honor and fatten their purses. Not only does control of additional companies add to personal income and perks, it multiplies the potential for building equity that will not be taxed until divestiture. (As of the writing of this book, some commentators believe that the Bush administration will reintroduce a favorable capital gains tax rate. Even if it does not, it is unlikely that the Bush administration will make it more burdensome to be a business owner in America.)

Not only are the times right for those who are able to undertake acquisitions, this book offers a pattern of advice that begs to be replicated.

By nature the advice in this book is expansionist, showing you how to acquire a bankrupt company at the lowest cost. You will not be relying on one secret or trick that will be easily rebuffed when discovered, but rather upon sound procedures for tapping into the "gold" languishing in bankruptcy court. By using this book as a touchstone, you can acquire a business or expand your own in a quantum leap.

Once you have done so, the same advice can then be applied again...and again...and again. The strategies and tactics that I have described can be applied to a wide range of circumstances. The opportunities in bankruptcy court are great and the competition minimal. Even if you become known as a bankruptcy court "regular" who is always on the prowl for new acquisitions, no one can stop you— and that reputation will only cause more opportunities to be laid on your platter!

If you have learned your lessons and have the right stuff, by all means start searching for a bankrupt company to acquire. When both this book and you have met the test and you have turned around the company that you have acquired, by all means go out and do it again.

Good hunting!

Glossary

Administrative Creditor—a party who is owed money by a Chapter 11 Debtor, the debt having arisen from the providing of goods or services to the Debtor during its Chapter 11 case.

Appearance—a court form that is filed with a court clerk by which an attorney formally states his representation of a party in a particular case, thereby submitting the attorney and the client to the jurisdiction of the court.

Assignment of Beneficial Interest—a security device that creates a lien upon the beneficial ownership of real estate that is held in a land trust. The lien thus created is considered to be upon personal property rather than upon real estate.

Automatic Stay—an injunction against creditor collection actions that goes into effect upon the filing of a petition by a Debtor without the need for a specific court order, irrespective of any actual notice to those creditors.

Balance Sheet—a statement by a business, in a generally accepted form, that lists its assets and liabilities as of a specific date.

Bankrupt—formerly, a party who was the subject of a bankruptcy case filed under Chapter 7; now obsolete, as under the bankruptcy code such a party is a "Debtor."

Bankruptcy Code—the comprehensive provisions enacted concurrently on November 6, 1978 that became effective on October 1, 1979, which provide the entire statutory authority for bankruptcy laws in the United States; the latest in a series of such comprehensive statutes that date back to the early 1800s, which completely superseded the "Bankruptcy Act" on October 1, 1979.

Bankruptcy Court—one of a nationwide system of federal courts of limited jurisdiction created to administer bankruptcy cases and to hear most of the disputes arising in those cases, which are subordinate to federal district courts of general jurisdiction.

Bankruptcy Judge—a federal judge appointed to preside in a bank-rutpcy court, who is subordinate to federal district court judges.

Bankruptcy Rules—a comprehensive set of rules promulgated by the United States Supreme Court under authority from Congress that clarifies the bankruptcy code and provides specific provisions for effectuating sections of the code.

Bar Date—*not* someone you met at a lounge; the final date on which a creditor may make a claim against a Debtor by filing it with the clerk of the bankruptcy court, claims not filed by the bar date becoming totally unenforceable.

Chapter 7—the portion of the bankruptcy code that establishes the procedures for the discharge of all of a Debtor's debts upon the payment to the Debtor's creditors of funds generated by the sale of all of the Debtor's nonexempt property owned on the date of the filing of the bankruptcy.

Chapter 11—the portion of the bankruptcy code that establishes the procedures for the discharge of all of a Debtor's debts upon payment to the Debtor's creditors pursuant to a Plan of Reorganization approved by the creditors and the bankruptcy judge presiding over the Debtor's bankruptcy case.

Collateral—property that is the subject of a lien created by a security agreement; the security provided by a borrower to a lender.

Confirmation—the finding by a bankruptcy judge that the requisite number of creditors have voted to approve a Plan of Reorganization and that it does not violate any prohibitions in the bankruptcy code.

Creditor—a party who claims to be owed money, including claiming an unliquidated debt (exact amount not determined yet) or a contingent liability (debt may arise upon the happening of an occurrence in the future).

Cost-of-Administration—an expense incurred for the benefit of a Debtor or as part of the ordinary administration of a bankruptcy case.

Debtor [with a capital "D"]—the party provided protection from creditors under the bankruptcy code as a result of a filing of a bankruptcy petition, as opposed to a "debtor" who is merely a party who owes a debt.

Debtor in Possession—a Chapter 11 Debtor that remains in possession of its property and is permitted to continue operating its business subject to limits established by bankruptcy law.

D.I.P.—a Debtor in Possession

Disclosure Statement—the written analysis of a Debtor's past and present operations, and a comparison of the dividend proposed to be paid to creditors versus that which they would receive in the event of liquidation, which, upon prior court approval, must be sent to all creditors along with the Plan of Reorganization; the document that is to contain sufficient information to enable creditors to decide whether to accept or reject a Plan of Reorganization.

Dividend—the payment to a creditor of a Debtor through the bank-ruptcy process.

Docket—a listing maintained by a court clerk that summarizes either (a) pleadings that have been filed and orders that have been entered, or (b) claims that have been filed, respecting a case.

Equity Security Holder—term utilized in the bankruptcy code for either a shareholder or a debentureholder; an owner of a corporation.

Exclusive Period—the time period during which the Chapter 11 Debtor has the exclusive right to file a Plan of Reorganization and/or acquire the approval of the creditors to that plan.

Goodwill—the positive feelings of customers and potential customers generated by providing a good product and/or services, which increase the likelihood that they will make purchases in the future from that same supplier.

Investor—a party who acquires an ownership interest in a company that is insufficient to provide control.

"Involuntary" Petition—a petition filed by creditors alleging that a debtor is insolvent and asking that the bankruptcy court take jurisdiction by declaring that debtor to be a Debtor.

Lien—the right to seize and sell property of another in the event of the default of an obligation, which may arise by voluntary agreement or by court decree and which may be limited to specific property or extended to all property owned by the debtor.

Liquidation—the conversion of property to cash through its forced sale; or, the fixing of the exact amount of a debt.

Mortgage—a security agreement that creates a lien upon real estate.

Operating Report—a form required to be filed by a Chapter 11 Debtor-in-Possession or a Chapter 11 trustee which describes income earned and expenses incurred for the prior month of business operations, and also contains a summary of accounts receivable and payable.

Petition—the one-page court form that asks that the subject person, partnership, or corporation be designated as a "Debtor" under the bankruptcy code, which becomes operative upon its filing with a clerk of a bankruptcy court.

Plan of Reorganization—a written proposal made to creditors pursuant to Chapter 11 of the bankruptcy code that provides for the discharge of all debts of a Debtor upon payment described therein.

Priority Creditor—a party that is owed money and is entitled to receive payment from a Debtor in bankruptcy prior to unsecured creditors due to a provision in the bankruptcy code which accords such preferred status; e.g., taxing bodies, and parties who have provided goods or services to the Debtor during a Chapter 11 case.

Profit/Loss Statement—a statement by a business, in a generally accepted form, that describes its income earned and expenses incurred (on an accrued basis), or its receipts and expenditures (on a cash basis), during a given period of time.

Purchaser—a party who acquires a controlling ownership interest in a company.

Schedules—technically, the "Schedules of Assets and Liabilities" filed by a Debtor; commonly, not only the aforementioned form but also including the "Statement of Financial Affairs for Debtor Engaged in Business," as they are generally filed at the same time and bound together.

Secured Creditor—a party that is owed money, and has acquired a lien upon property to secure payment.

Security Agreement—a voluntary contract entered into to provide a creditor with a lien upon property of another.

Security Interest—a lien.

Stay—an injunction; a court imposed prohibition against taking a specific action.

Trustee—a person having no previous connection with a Debtor who is appointed to administer the Debtor's assets, and who liquidates the nonexempt property and pays the creditors of a Chapter 7 Debtor or preserves the assets (including operating the business, if appropriate) of a Chapter 11 Debtor; not to be confused with a United States Trustee.

United States Trustee—an employee of the United States who, personally or through assistants, is charged by the bankruptcy code with holding the initial meeting of creditors upon the filing of a Chapter 11 case, appointing members of Unsecured Creditors' Committees and other committees authorized by a court, appointing trustees to administer Debtors' assets, supervising trustees' activities, and seeing to it that Debtors perform their obligations under the bankruptcy code.

Unsecured Creditor—a party that is owed money, holding a debt that is neither secured by a lien nor classified by law as having priority in payment.

Appendices

APPENDIX A

SCHEDULES OF ASSETS AND LIABILITIES

UNITED STATES BANKRUPTCY COURT FOR THE

. . . . DISTRICT OF . . . .

In re

. . . . ,

Case No. . . . .

Debtor [set forth here all names including trade names used by Debtor within last 6 years].

Social Security Number . . . .

and Debtor's Employer's Tax Identification No. . . . .

Schedule A — Statement of All Liabilities of Debtor.

Schedules A-1, A-2, and A-3 must include all the claims against the debtor or his property as of the date of the filing of the petition by or against him.

Schedule A—1. — Creditors having priority.

Nature of claim.	Name of creditor and complete mailing address including zip code.	Specify when claim was incurred and the consideration therefor; when claim is subject to setoff, evidenced by a judgment, negotiable instrument, or other writing, or incurred as partner or joint contractor, so indicate; specify name of any partner or joint contractor on any debt.	Indicate if claim is contingent, unliquidated, or disputed.	Amount of claim.
a. Wages, salary, and commissions, including vacation, severance and sick leave pay owing to employees not exceeding $2,000 to each, earned within 90 days before filing of petition or cessation of business (if earlier specify date).				$
b. Contributions to employee benefit plans for services rendered within 180 days before filing of petition or cessation of business (if earlier specify date).				
c. Deposits by individuals, not exceeding $900 for each for purchase, lease, or rental of property or services for personal, family, or household use that were not delivered or provided.				
d. Taxes owing [itemize by type of tax and taxing authority]. (1) To the United States (2) To any state (3) To any other taxing authority				

Total

Schedule A-2 — Creditors Holding Security.

Name of creditor and complete mailing address including zip code	Description of security and date when obtained by creditor	Specify when claim was incurred and the consideration therefor, when claim is subject to setoff, evidenced by a judgment, negotiable instrument, or other writing, or incurred as partner or joint contractor, so indicate; specify name of any partner or joint contractor on any debt.	Indicate if claim is contingent, unliquidated, or disputed.	Market value	Amount of claim without deduction of value of security
				$	$
			Total		

Schedule A-3 — Creditors having unsecured claims without priority.

Name of creditor (including last known holder of any negotiable instrument) and complete mailing address including zip code.	Specify when claim was incurred and the consideration therefor, when claim is contingent, unliquidated, disputed, subject to setoff, evidenced by a judgment, negotiable instrument, or other writing, or incurred as partner or joint contractor, so indicate, specify name of any partner or joint contractor on any debt	Indicate if claim is contingent, unliquidated, or disputed	Amount of claim
			$
		Total	

Schedule B — Statement of All Property of Debtor

Schedules B-1, B-2, B-3 and B-4 must include all property of the debtor as of the date of the filing of the petition by or against him.

Schedule B-1. — Real Property

Description and location of all real property in which debtor has an interest [including equitable and future interests, interests in estates by the entirety, community property, life estates, leaseholds, and rights and powers exercisable for his own benefit]	Nature of interest [specify all deeds and written instruments relating thereto]	Market value of debtor's interest without deduction for secured claims listed in Schedule A-2 or exemptions claimed in Schedule B-4
		$
		Total

Schedule B-2 — Personal Property

Type of Property	Description and Location	Market value of debtor's interest without deduction for secured claims listed on Schedule A-2 or exemptions claimed in Schedule B-4
a. Cash on hand		$
b. Deposits of money with banking institutions, savings and loan associations, brokerage houses, credit unions, public utility companies, landlords and others		
c. Household goods, supplies and furnishings		
d. Books, pictures, and other art objects; stamp, coin and other collections		
e. Wearing apparel, jewelry, firearms, sports equipment and other personal possessions		
f. Automobiles, trucks, trailers and other vehicles		
g. Boats, motors and their accessories		
h. Livestock, poultry and other animals		
i. Farming equipment, supplies and implements		
j. Office equipment, furnishings and supplies		
Machinery, fixtures, equipment and supplies [other than those listed in Items j and l] used in business		
l. Inventory		
m. Tangible personal property of any other description		
n. Patents, copyrights, licenses, franchises and other general intangibles [specify all documents and writings relating thereto]		
o. Government and corporate bonds and other negotiable and nonnegotiable instruments		
p. Other liquidated debts owing debtor		
q. Contingent and unliquidated claims of every nature, including counterclaims of the debtor [give estimated value of each]		
r. Interests in insurance policies [name insurance company of each policy and itemize surrender or refund value of each]		
s. Annuities [itemize and name each issuer]		
t. Stock and interests in incorporated and unincorporated companies [itemize separately]		
u. Interests in partnerships		
v. Equitable and future interests, life estates, and rights or powers exercisable for the benefit of the debtor (other than those listed in Schedule B-1) [specify all written instruments relating thereto]		

Total

Schedule B-3. — Property not otherwise scheduled

Type of property	Description and location	Market value of debtor's interest without deduction for secured claims listed in Schedule A-2 or exemption claimed in Schedule B-4
a. Property transferred under assignment for benefit of creditors, within 120 days prior to filing of petition [specify date of assignment, name and address of assignee, amount realized therefrom by the assignee, and disposition of proceeds so far as known to debtor]		$
b. Property of any kind not otherwise scheduled		
	Total	

Debtor selects the following property as exempt pursuant to 11 U.S.C. § 522(d) [or the laws of the State of . . . .]

Schedule B-4. — Property claimed as exempt

Type of property	Location, description, and, so far as relevant to the claim of exemption, present use of property	Specify statute creating the exemption	Value claimed exempt
			$

Total

Summary of debts and property.

[From the statements of the debtor in Schedules A and B]

Schedule		Total
	DEBTS	$
A-1/a,b	Wages, etc. having priority	
A-1(c)	Deposits of money	
A-1/d(1)	Taxes owing United States	
A-1/d(2)	Taxes owing states	
A-1/d(3)	Taxes owing other taxing authorities	
A-2	Secured claims	
A-3	Unsecured claims without priority	
	Schedule A Total	
	PROPERTY	
B-1	Real property [total value]	
B-2/a	Cash on hand	
B-2/b	Deposits	
B-2/c	Household goods	
B-2/d	Books, pictures, and collections	
B-2/e	Wearing apparel and personal possessions	
B-2/f	Automobiles and other vehicles	
B-2/g	Boats, motors, and accessories	
B-2/h	Livestock and other animals	
B-2/i	Farming supplies and implements	
B-2/j	Office equipment and supplies	
B-2/k	Machinery, equipment, and supplies used in business	
B-2/l	Inventory	
/m	Other tangible personal property	
B-2/n	Patents and other general intangibles	
B-2/o	Bonds and other instruments	
B-2/p	Other liquidated debts	
B-2/q	Contingent and unliquidated claims	
B-2/r	Interests in insurance policies	
B-2/s	Annuities	
B-2/t	Interests in corporations and unincorporated companies	
B-2/u	Interests in partnerships	
B-2/v	Equitable and future interests, rights, and powers in personalty	
B-3/a	Property assigned for benefit of creditors	
B-3/b	Property not otherwise scheduled	
	Schedule B total	

Unsworn Declaration under Penalty of Perjury
on Behalf of Corporation or Partnership
to Schedules A and B

I, ... , (the president or other officer or an authorized agent of the corporation) (or a member or an authorized agent of the partnership) named as debtor in this case, declare under penalty of perjury that I have read the foregoing schedules, consisting of . . . . . sheets, and that they are true and correct to the best of my knowledge, information and belief.

Executed on . . . .

Signature: . . . .

APPENDIX B

STATEMENT OF FINANCIAL AFFAIRS FOR DEBTOR ENGAGED IN BUSINESS

UNITED STATES BANKRUPTCY COURT FOR THE

. . . . DISTRICT OF . . . .

x

In re

:

. . . . ,

:   Case No. . . . .

Debtor [set forth here all names including trade names used by Debtor within last 6 years]

:

Social Security Number . . . .

:

and Debtor's Employer's Tax Identification No. . . . .

x

Statement of Financial Affairs for Debtor Engaged in Business

[Each question shall be answered or the failure to answer explained. If the answer is "none" or "not applicable," so state. If additional space is needed for the answer to any question, a separate sheet properly identified and made a part hereof, should be used and attached.

If the debtor is a partnership or a corporation, the questions shall be deemed to be addressed to, and shall be answered on behalf of, the partnership or corporation; and the statement shall be certified by a member of the partnership or by a duly authorized officer of the corporation.

The term, "original petition," used in the following questions, shall mean the petition filed under Rule 1002, 1003, or 1004.]

1. Nature, location, and name of business

a. Under what name and where do you carry on your business?

b. In what business are you engaged? (If business operations have been terminated, give the date of termination.)

c. When did you commence the business?

d. Where else, and under what other names, have you carried on business within the six years immediately preceding the filing of the original petition herein? (Give street addresses, the names of any partners, joint adventurers, or other associates, the nature of the business, and the periods for which it was carried on.)

2. Books and records.

a. By whom, or under whose supervision, have your books of account and records been kept during the six years immediately preceding the filing of the original petition herein? (Give names, addresses, and periods of time.)

b. By whom have your books of account and records been audited during the six years immediately preceding the filing of the original petition herein? (Give names, addresses, and dates of audits.)

c. In whose possession are your books of account and records? (Give names and addresses.)

d. If any of these books or records are not available, explain.

e. Have any books of account or records relating to your affairs been destroyed, lost, or otherwise disposed of within the two years immediately preceding the filing of the original petition herein? (If so, give particulars, including date of destruction, loss, or disposition, and reason therefor.)

3. Financial statements.

Have you issued any written financial statements within the two years immediately preceding the filing of the original petition herein? (Give dates, and the name and addresses of the persons to whom issued, including mercantile and trade agencies.)

4. Inventories.

a. When was the last inventory of your property taken?

b. By whom, or under whose supervision, was this inventory taken?

c. What was the amount, in dollars, of the inventory? (State whether the inventory was taken as cost, market, or otherwise.)

d. When was the next prior inventory of your property taken?

e. By whom, or under whose supervision, was this inventory taken?

f. What was the amount, in dollars, of the inventory? (State whether the inventory was taken at cost, market, or otherwise.)

g. In whose possession are the records of the two inventories above referred to? (Give names and addresses.)

5. Income other than from operation of business.

What amount of income, other than from operation of your business, have you received during each of the two years immediately preceding the filing of the original petition herein? (Give particulars, including each source, and the amount received therefrom.)

6. Tax returns and refunds.

a. In whose possession are copies of your federal, state and municipal income tax returns for the three years immediately preceding the filing of the original petition herein?

b. What tax refunds (income or other) have you received during the two years immediately preceding the filing of the original petition herein?

c. To what tax refunds (income or other), if any, are you, or may you be, entitled? (Give particulars, including information as to any refund payable jointly to you and your spouse or any other person.)

7. Financial accounts, certificates of deposit and safe deposit boxes.

a. What accounts or certificates of deposit or shares in banks, savings and loan, thrift, building and loan and homestead associations, credit unions, brokerage houses, pension funds and the like have you maintained, alone or together with any other person, and in your own or any other name, within the two years immediately preceding the filing of the original petition herein? (Give the name and address of each institution, the name and number under which the account of certificate is maintained, and the name and address of every person authorized to make withdrawals from such account.)

b. What safe deposit box or boxes or other depository or depositories have you kept or used for your securities, cash, or other valuables within the two years immediately preceding the filing of the original petition herein? (Give the name and address of the bank or other depository, the name in which each box or other depository was kept, the name and address of every person who had the right of access thereto, a description of the contents thereof, and, if the box has been surrendered, state when surrendered or, if transferred, when transferred, and the name and address of the transferee.)

8. Property held for another person.

What property do you hold for any other person? (Give name and address of each person, and describe the property, the amount or value thereof and all writings relating thereto.)

9. Property held by another person.

Is any other person holding anything of value in which you have an interest? (Give name and address, location and description of the property, and circumstances of the holding.)

10. Prior bankruptcy proceedings.

What cases under the bankruptcy Act or title 11, United States Code have previously been brought by or against you? (State the location of the bankruptcy court, the nature and number of the case, and whether a discharge was granted or denied, the case was dismissed, or a composition, arrangement, or plan was confirmed.)

11. Receiverships, general assignments, and other modes of liquidation.

a. Was any of your property, at the time of the filing of the original petition herein, in the hands of a receiver, trustee, or other liquidating agent? (If so, give a brief description of the property and the name and address of the receiver, trustee, or other agent, if the agent was appointed in a court proceeding, the name and location of the court, the title and number of the case, and the nature thereof.)

b. Have you made any assignment of your property for the benefit of your creditors, or any general settlement with your creditors, within the two years immediately preceding the filing of the original petition herein? (If so, give dates, the name and address of the assignee, and a brief statement of the terms of assignment or settlement.)

12. Suits, executions, and attachments.

a. Were you a party to any suit pending at the time of the filing of the original petition herein? (If so, give the name and location of the court and the title and nature of the proceeding.)

b. Were you a party to any suit terminated within the year immediately preceding the filing of the original petition herein? (If so, give the name and location of the court, the title and nature of the proceeding, and the result.)

c. Has any of your property been attached, garnished, or seized under any legal or equitable process within the year immediately preceding the filing of the original petition herein? (If so, describe the property seized or person garnished, and at whose suit.)

13. a. Payments of loans, installment purchases and other debts.

What payments in whole or in part have you made during the year immediately preceding the filing of the original petition herein on any of the following: (1) loans; (2) installment purchases of goods and services; and (3) other debts? (Give the names and addresses of the persons receiving payment, the amounts of the loans or other debts and of the purchase price of the goods and services, the dates of the original transactions, the amounts and dates of payments, and, if any of the payees are your relatives or insiders, the relationship; if the debtor is a partnership and any of the payees is or was a partner or a relative of a partner, state the relationship; if the debtor is a corporation and any of the payees is or was an officer, director, or stockholder, or a relative of an officer, director, or stockholder, state the relationship.)

b. Setoffs.

What debts have you owed to any creditor, including any bank, which were setoff by that creditor against a debt or deposit owing by the creditor to you during the year immediately preceding the filing of the original petition herein? (Give the names and addresses of the persons setting off such debts, the dates of the setoffs, the amounts of the debts owing by you and to you and, if any of the creditors are your relatives or insiders, the relationship.)

14. Transfers of property.

a. Have you made any gifts, other than ordinary and usual presents to family members and charitable donations during the year immediately preceding the filing of the original petition herein? (If so, give names and addresses of donees and dates, description, and value of gifts.)

b. Have you made any other transfer, absolute or for the purpose of security, or any other disposition which was not in the ordinary course of business during the year immediately preceding the filing of the original petition herein? (Give a description of the property, the date of the transfer or disposition, to whom transferred or how disposed of, and state whether the transferee is a relative, partner, shareholder, officer, director or insider, the consideration, if any, received for the property, and the disposition of such consideration.)

15. Accounts and other receivables.

Have you assigned, either absolutely or as security, any of your accounts or other receivables during the year immediately preceding the filing of the original petition herein? (If so, give names and addresses of assignees.)

16. Repossessions and returns.

Has any property been returned to, or repossessed by, the seller, lessor, or a secured party during the year immediately preceding the filing of the original petition herein? (If so, give particulars, including the name and address of the party getting the property and its description and value.)

17. Business leases.

If you are a tenant of business property, what is the name and address of your landlord, the amount of your rental, the date to which rent had been paid at the time of the filing of the original petition herein, and the amount of security held by the landlord?

18. Losses.

. Have you suffered any losses from fire, theft, or gambling during .he year immediately preceding the filing of the original petiton herein? (If so, give particulars, including dates, names, and places, and the amounts of money or value and general description of property lost.)

b. Was the loss covered in whole or part by insurance? (If so, give particulars.)

19. Withdrawals.

a. If you are an individual proprietor of your business, what personal withdrawals of any kind have you made from the business during the year immediately preceding the filing of the original petition herein?

b. If the debtor is a partnership or corporation, what withdrawals, in any form (including compensation, bonuses or loans), have been made or received by any member of the partnership, or by any officer, director, insider, managing executive, or shareholder of the corporation, during the year immediately preceding the filing of the original petition herein? (Give the name and designation or relationship to the debtor of each person, the dates and amounts of withdrawals, and the nature or purpose thereof.)

20. Payments or tranfers to attorneys.

a. Have you consulted an attorney during the year immediately preceding or since the filing of the original petition herein? (Give date, name, and address.)

b. Have you during the year immediately preceding or since the filing of the original petition herein paid any money or transferred any property to the attorney, or to any other person on his behalf? (If so, give particulars, including amount paid or value of property transferred and date of payment or transfer.)

c. Have you, either during the year immediately preceding or since the filing of the original petition herein, agreed to pay any money or transfer any property to an attorney at law, or to any other person on his behalf? (If so, give particulars, including amount and terms of obligation.)

(If the debtor is a partnership or corporation, the following additional questions should be answered.)

21. Members of partnership; officers, directors, managers, and principal stockholders of corporation.

a. What is the name and address of each member of the partnership, or the name, title, and address of each officer, director, insider, and managing executive, and of each stockholder holding 20 percent or more of the issued and outstanding stock, of the corporation?

b. During the year immediately preceding the filing of the original petition herein, has any member withdrawn from the partnership, or any officer, director, insider, or managing executive of the corporation terminated his relationship, or any stockholder holding 20 percent or more of the issued stock disposed of more than 50 percent of his holdings? (If so, give name and address and reason for withdrawal, termination, or disposition, if known.)

c. Has any person acquired or disposed of 20 percent or more of the stock of the corporation during the year immediately preceding the filing of the petition? (If so, give name and address and particulars.)

I, ..., declare under penalty of perjury that I have read the answers contained in the foregoing statement of affairs and that they are true and correct to the best of my knowledge, information, and belief

Executed on . . . .

Signature: . . . .

APPENDIX C

IN THE UNITED STATES BANKRUPTCY COURT
FOR THE NORTHERN DISTRICT OF ILLINOIS
EASTERN DIVISION

IN RE:)
)
)
) CASE NO.
)
) Debtor in Possession (DIP) Operating
) Report-Summary of Cash Receipts
) and Disbursements; Statements of
) Aged Payables and Receivables
)
     Debtor(s).)

Employer Identification No. or   Monthly Report No. _____
Social Security No.   For the period ending

_____   _____ , 198__

Beginning Cash Balance in DIP General Account............ $_____

RECEIPTS:
 1. Receipts from Operations......... $_____
 2. *Other Receipts.................. $_____

   TOTAL RECEIPTS................... $_____

DISBURSEMENTS:
 3. Net Payroll:
  a. Officers..................... $_____
  b. Others....................... $_____
 4. Taxes:
  a. Federal Withholding.......... $_____
  b. Employer FICA Contribution... $_____
  c. Illinois Withholding......... $_____
  d. Real Estate.................. $_____
  e. Sales........................ $_____
  f. Other........................ $_____
 5. Necessary Expenses
  a. Rent......................... $_____
  b. Utilities.................... $_____
  c. Insurance.................... $_____
  d. Merchandise bought for
   manufacture or sale.......... $_____
  e. *Other Necessary Expenses..... $_____

   TOTAL DISBURSEMENTS.............. $_____

NET RECEIPTS (DISBURSEMENTS) FOR THE CURRENT PERIOD...... $_____

Ending Cash Balance in DIP General Account............... $_____

* Itemize on separate sheet if material.

STATEMENT OF AGED RECEIVABLES

STATEMENT OF ACCOUNTS RECEIVABLE

On Hand at Beginning of Month............... $_____
Plus: Sales on Account .... $_____
Less: Collections........................... $_____
On Hand at End of Month.................... $_____

	0-30 days	31-60 days	61-90 days	Over 90 days	Total Due
TOTALS	$_____	$_____	$_____	$_____	$_____

PREPARE SCHEDULE OF AGED RECEIVABLES IF NECESSARY (See attached)

STATEMENT OF AGED PAYABLES

STATEMENT OF ACCOUNTS PAYABLE

On Hand at Beginning of Month............... $_____
Plus: Credit Extended....................... $_____
Less: Payments on Account................... $_____
On Hand at End of Month.................... $_____

	0-30 days	31-60 days	61-90 days	Over 90 days	Total Due
TOTALS	$_____	$_____	$_____	$_____	$_____

PREPARE SCHEDULE OF AGED PAYABLES IF NECESSARY (See attached)

PREPARE SCHEDULE OF STATUS OF PAYMENTS TO SECURED CREDITORS
AND LESSORS IF NECESSARY (See attached)

VERIFICATION:

I declare under penalty of perjury that the information contained in
the foregoing Operating Reports and the schedules attached thereto is true
and correct to the best of my knowledge.

_____   _____
DATE   DESIGNATED REPRESENTATIVE

SCHEDULE OF AGED RECEIVABLES

Name of Account	31-60 days	61-90 days	Over 90 days	Total

	31-60 days	61-90 days	Over 90 days	Total
SUBTOTALS	$_____	$_____	$_____	$_____
ESTIMATED BAD DEBTS (IN DOLLARS)	$_____	$_____	$_____	$_____
TOTAL COLLECTIBLE	$_____	$_____	$_____	$_____

SCHEDULE OF STATUS OF PAYMENTS
TO SECURED CREDITORS AND LESSORS

Creditor/ Lessor	When Payments Due (i.e. Monthly, Quarterly)	Amount Of Each Regular Payment	Number of Post-Petition Payments Delinquent	Amount of Post-Petition Payments Delinquent	Next Payment Due

APPENDIX D

United States Bankruptcy Court

For the_____ District of_____

In re

Case No._____

Debtor*

PROOF OF CLAIM

1. [*If claimant is an individual claiming for himself*] The undersigned, who is the claimant herein, resides at**

[*If claimant is a partnership claiming through a member*] The undersigned, who resides at**

is a member of _____ , a partnership,
composed of the undersigned and
of** , and
doing business at**
and is authorized to make this proof of claim on behalf of the partnership.

    [*If claimant is a corporation claiming through an authorized officer*] The undersigned, who resides at**

is the of
a corporation organized under the laws of
and doing business at**
and is authorized to make this proof of claim on behalf of the corporation.

    [*If claim is made by agent*] The undersigned, who resides at**
, is the agent of
, of** , and is
authorized to make this proof of claim on behalf of the claimant.

    2. The debtor was, at the time of the filing of the petition initiating this case, and still is indebted [or liable] to this claimant, in the sum of $

    3. The consideration for this debt [or ground of liability] is as follows:

    4. [*If the claim is founded on writing*] The writing on which this claim is founded (or a duplicate thereof) is attached here to [or cannot be attached for the reason set forth in the statement attached hereto].
$

If appropriate] This claim is founded on an open account, which became [or will become] due on
, as shown by the itemized statement attached hereto..
Unless it is attached hereto or its absence is explained in an attached statement, no note or other negotiable instrument has been received for the account or any part of it.

    6. No judgment has been rendered on the claim except

    7. The amount of all payments of this claim has been credited and deducted for the purpose of making this proof of claim.

    8. This claim is not subject to any setoff or counter-claim except

    9. No security interest is held for this claim except

[*If security interest in property of the debtor is claimed*] The undersigned claims the security interest under the writing referred to in paragraph 4 hereof [or under a separate writing which (or a duplicate of which) is attached hereto, or under a separate writing which cannot be attached hereto for the reason set forth in the statement attached hereto]. Evidence of perfection of such security interest is also attached hereto.

    10. This claim is a general unsecured claim, except to the extent that the security interest, if any, described in paragraph 9 is sufficient to satisfy the claim. [*If priority is claimed, state the amount and basis thereof.*]

                     (Unsecured)
    11. This claim is filed as a (n) (Secured)   CLAIM.
                     (Priority)

$_____
Total Amount Claimed

Claim Number
(For Office Use Only)

Name of Creditor:_____
(Print or Type Full Name of Creditor)

Dated: Signed:_____

Penalty for Presenting Fraudulent Claim. Fine of not more than $5,000 or imprisonment for not more than 5 years or both-Title 18. U.S.C.. §152.

*Include all names used by Debtor within last 6 years.
**State post office address..

APPENDIX E

IN THE UNITED STATES BANKRUPTCY COURT
FOR THE NORTHERN DISTRICT OF ILLINOIS
EASTERN DIVISION

IN RE:	)	
	)	
WIDGET MANUFACTURING	)	NO. 88 B 0000
CORPORATION,	)	
	)	
Debtor	)	
	)	

DEBTOR'S PLAN OF REORGANIZATION

Now comes WIDGET MANUFACTURING CORPORATION, an Illinois corporation and the Debtor in this proceeding, and proposes to its creditors the following Plan of Reorganization for the payment of its indebtedness and the modification and alteration of the rights of its creditors.

ARTICLE I

DEFINITIONS

The following terms, when used in this Plan of Reorganization shall, unless the context otherwise requires, have the following meanings, respectively:

1. <u>Bankruptcy Code</u>: The United States Bankruptcy Code, 11 USC Section 101 <u>et</u> <u>seq</u>.

2. <u>Committee</u>: The committee of unsecured creditors constituted pursuant to Section 1102 of the Bankruptcy Code as it now exists or as hereinafter reconstituted.

3. <u>Plan</u>: This Plan of Reorganization.

4.   <u>Court</u>:   The United States Bankruptcy Court for the
     Northern   District   of   Illinois,   Eastern   Division,
     presiding over the Debtor's Chapter 11 proceeding.

5.   <u>Confirmation</u>:   The entry of a final Order of the Court
     confirming the Plan in accordance with Chapter 11 of
     the Bankruptcy Code.

6.   <u>Debtor</u>:   Widget Manufacturing Corporation, an Illinois
     Corporation.

7.   <u>Effective Date of the Plan</u>:   Ten days after the Order
     of   Confirmation   becomes   a   final   order,   unless
     effectuation of the Plan has been stayed by a Court
     order.

<u>ARTICLE II</u>

<u>CLASSIFICATION OF CLAIMS AND INTERESTS</u>

<u>Class 1</u>

Allowed administrative claims entitled to priority pursuant
to the provisions of Section 507(a)(1) through 507(a)(6) of the
Bankruptcy Code.

<u>Class 2</u>

All other claims incurred by the Debtor-in-Possession from
the date of the filing of the bankruptcy petition through the
date of the entry of an order confirming the Plan.

<u>Class 3</u>

Allowed tax claims entitled to priority pursuant to the
provisions of Section 507(a)(7) of the Bankruptcy Code.

<u>Class 4</u>

Allowed claim of Last National Bank ("the Bank").

Class 5

Allowed unsecured claims of $300 or less, and those unsecured claims allowed in excess of $300 that are voluntarily reduced to $300 by the claimants on or before the last date for voting upon the Plan.

Class 6.

Allowed unsecured claims not otherwise classified herein.

Class 7

Interests of the holders of the Debtor's stock.

ARTICLE III

CLAIMS AND INTERESTS NOT IMPAIRED UNDER THE PLAN

Class 1 and Class 5 claims shall remain unaltered, and shall be paid in full in cash upon the Effective Date of the Plan.

Class 2 claims shall remain unaltered, and each shall be paid when it shall become due.

Class 7 interests shall remain unaltered, but shall not be paid pursuant to this Plan.

ARTICLE IV

TREATMENT OF CLASSES THAT ARE IMPAIRED UNDER THE PLAN

All Class 3 claims shall be paid in full, with statutory interest, over a period or at such other time as may be allowed under Section 1129(a)(9)(c) of the Bankruptcy Code unless the holder of such claim consents to such claim being treated differently.

As to the Class 4 claim , on the Effective Date of the Plan the Bank shall receive an Installment Promissory Note ("the Note") in the amount of $1,000,000, substantially in the form attached hereto as Exhibit A. Upon receipt of said Note the Bank's claim shall be satisfied in full, except to the extent evidenced by the Note.

Each Class 6 claim shall be fully satisfied and discharged upon receipt by the holder thereof of a pro rata share of the Class 6 claims of the payment of $100,000 to be provided by the Debtor. Said $100,000 shall be deposited within 30 days of the Effective Date of the Plan in a checking account, and shall be distributed by the Debtor to the Class 6 creditors pursuant to this paragraph within 14 days of the date on which all Class 6 claims shall be determined and allowed.

ARTICLE V

PROVISIONS RE EXECUTORY CONTRACTS AND UNEXPIRED LEASES

Attached hereto as Exhibit B is a listing of the Debtor's executory contracts and unexpired leases, each of which shall be deemed assumed on the Effective Date of the Plan.

ARTICLE VI
MEANS OF EXECUTION

OF THE PLAN

All funds necessary for the payment of the claims of Classes 1, 5, and 6 shall be acquired by the Debtor upon the Effective Date of the Plan pursuant to investment in the Debtor by Mr. Cash Angel. All funds necessary for the payment of the claims of Classes 2, 3, and 4 shall be created by the Debtor's cash flow in the ordinary course of its future operations.

ARTICLE VII

FUTURE MANAGEMENT OF THE DEBTOR

Cash Angel as President and Treasurer, and Cash Angel II as Vice-President and Secretary,   shall assume such positions upon the Effective Date of the Plan.

ARTICLE VIII

MODIFICATIONS OF THE PLAN

The Debtor may propose amendments of modifications of this Plan at any time prior to Confirmation, with approval of the Court, upon notice to creditors if the change is material. After Confirmation the Debtor may, with approval of the Court and so long as it does not materially or adversely affect the interests of creditors, remedy any defect or omission, or reconcile any inconsistencies in the Plan or in the Order of Confirmation, in such manner as may be necessary to carry out the purposes of the Plan.

ARTICLE IX

JURISDICTION OF THE COURT

Upon Confirmation, the Court shall retain jurisdiction over the Debtor for the limited purpose of determining objections that may be made by the Debtor to the claims filed in this proceeding, and insuring that the distributions to be made to creditors are made in accordance with the terms of the Plan. Unless and to the extent that the Court is called upon by the Debtor, a creditor of the Debtor, or other party in interest, to rule on an objection to a claim filed herein or to take some action to insure that the Debtor is complying with the Plan, upon Confirmation the Debtor may commence operating its business without Court supervision or control. Upon completion of the Debtor's undertakings under the Plan, the Debtor's Chapter 11 proceeding shall be terminated.

Dated:

WIDGET MANUFACTURING
CORPORATION

BY:_____
     One of Its Attorneys

Laurence H. Kallen
7500 Sears Tower
Chicago, Illinois
(312)876-7100

APPENDIX F

BALLOT FOR ACCEPTING OR REJECTING PLAN

[Caption   ]

BALLOT FOR ACCEPTING OR REJECTING PLAN

Filed by _____ on _____

The plan referred to in this ballot can be confirmed by the court and thereby made binding on you if it is accepted by the holders of two-thirds in amount and more than one-half in number of claims in each class and the holders of two-thirds in amount of equity security interests in each class voting on the plan. In the event the requisite acceptances are not obtained, the court may nevertheless confirm the plan if the court finds that the plan accords fair and equitable treatment to the class rejecting it. To have your vote count you must complete and return this ballot.

[If equity security holder] The undersigned, the holder of [state number] _____ shares of [describe type] stock of the above-named debtor, represented by Certificate(s) No.____, registered in the name of _____.

[If bondholder, debenture holder, or other debt security holder] The undersigned, the holder of [state unpaid principal amount] $_____of [describe security] of the above-named debtor, with a stated maturity date of [if applicable registered in the name of _____] [if applicable bearing serial number(s) _____.]

[If holder of general claim] The undersigned, a creditor of the above-named debtor in the unpaid principal amount of $_____.

[Check One Box]

☐ Accepts

☐ Rejects

the plan for the reorganization of the above-named debtor.

[If more than one plan is accepted, the following may not need be completed. The undersigned prefers the plans accepted in the following ordre: [Identify plans]

1. _____

2. _____

Dated: _____

Print or type name:

Signed:_____
        [If appropriate]

BY:_____

as:_____

Address:_____

_____

Return this ballot on or before _____

to:_____

_____

Index